The Primate Principle

Allen Schery

Brooklyn Bridge Books

Brooklyn Bridge Books

Contents

Chapter One

The First Bite: Why Chimps Steal Bananas

Imagine a ripe, yellow banana. It hangs tantalizingly from a branch, its skin glowing with the promise of sweet energy, an undeniable beacon of sustenance. Now, imagine a chimpanzee. He wants that banana. Badly. What does he do in that moment of undeniable craving? Does he pause, perhaps, to consider the intricate ethical implications of ownership, questioning whether the tree's bounty truly belongs to him, or to the collective, or perhaps exclusively to the chimp who might have spotted it first? Does he weigh the immediate gratification of his individual desire against some abstract notion of the troop's communal good, pondering whether taking it might somehow upset a fragile social balance? Does he even bother to consult a mental code of conduct, debating whether snatching it might violate a primal jungle equivalent of "fair play" or established property rights, concepts we humans hold so dear?

No. He simply calculates the leap. His eyes, sharp and intelligent, scan the environment, assessing the distance to the branch, gauging its probable strength to bear his weight, and, crucially, anticipating the possible reactions of nearby rivals or potential allies. He considers the immediate, tangible risk: is the branch too thin, threatening a dangerous fall? Is a larger, more dominant chimp watching, ready to assert its own superior claim through

1

brute force? If a smaller, less assertive chimp is already reaching for it, he might, without a flicker of remorse, empathy, or hesitation, shove them violently out of the way, or emit a threatening bark, asserting his superior claim through sheer intimidation. If the banana is already clutched in another's grasp, he might resort to sophisticated cunning—creating a sudden, loud diversion that draws attention away, then snatching it with lightning speed the moment their back is turned. Or, if the stakes are high enough, and the banana sufficiently prized to warrant significant effort, he might engage in a brutal, no-holds-barred fight, teeth bared, muscles tensed, until one combatant yields and the undisputed victor claims the prize. He takes it not because he has a moral right, but because he desires it and possesses the means—the strength, the agility, the cunning—to acquire it. The banana is the immediate prize, and the method to acquire it is dictated solely by opportunity, strength, and cunning, never by a code of conduct written on a stone tablet or an internal sense of universal fairness. His actions aren't immoral, for that implies a violation of a known code; they are, quite simply, amoral, existing in a realm where morality is utterly irrelevant.

Now, look in the mirror.

That's the profoundly uncomfortable truth this book dares you to confront. We, the ostensibly "naked apes," like to think of ourselves as fundamentally different from that chimp. We believe we are creatures elevated by the power of sophisticated reason, by a profound capacity for empathy, and, perhaps most importantly, by a deeply ingrained sense of morality. We construct intricate legal systems that dictate right from wrong, write voluminous codes of conduct that attempt to govern every conceivable interaction, engage in fervent philosophical and theological debates about justice and ethics, and summarily castigate those who "steal," cheat, or betray our established norms. We meticulously cultivate an elaborate self-image as stewards of justice, champions of fairness, and beacons of compassion. We eagerly point fingers at others for their perceived greed, their brazen ruthlessness, their blatant disregard for the common good. We build towering institutions, from global charities to ancient churches, ostensibly dedicated to promoting altruism and curbing self-interest, convinced they reflect an inherent human drive towards betterment. Our history books are meticulously filled with narratives of moral progress, of humanity striving, often heroically, towards a more just, equitable, and enlightened existence, each step forward a testament to our moral evolution.

Yet, peel back the layers. Strip away the bespoke suits and the sleek smartphones, the profound philosophies and the polite cocktail conversations that define our civilized veneer. Look beneath the grand pronouncements and the carefully constructed social rituals. What you will find are the same primal impulses that drive the chimp for his banana, still hardwired into our very being, albeit expressed with unparalleled complexity. Every international conflict fought over resources, every cutthroat corporate takeover, every intricate political maneuver, every deeply personal relationship struggle, every relentless and often unfulfilled craving for more – it all boils down, at its fundamental core, to an evolved, extraordinarily complex form of banana acquisition. The currency may be different, the methods more subtle, the justifications infinitely more elaborate, but the underlying drive remains astonishingly consistent. It is the inherent, relentless pursuit and acquisition of resources, power, and status, often—and inevitably—at the expense of others, always without an intrinsic moral compass truly guiding the action, only rationalizing it.

Let's be unequivocally clear about what "amoral" signifies in this context, for it is the linchpin of our argument. It does not mean "immoral." To be immoral implies a conscious violation of an existing moral code, a deliberate transgression against established rules of right and wrong, a choice to commit evil. The chimp, when it snatches a banana from a weaker peer, is not immoral; it simply operates entirely outside the realm of morality because such a framework simply does not exist for it. Similarly, our most fundamental, deeply ingrained drives are amoral. They are not born from a choice between good and evil, but are adaptive responses forged over millennia of brutal, unforgiving evolution, designed exclusively to ensure two paramount outcomes: survival and propagation. The acquisition of "bananas"—broadly defined to encompass everything from basic sustenance to profound influence—is merely the most effective means to these ends. Our drives are "a-moral," meaning "without morals," not "anti-moral." They are the raw, unthinking engine of our very being, operating in a sphere where concepts of good and evil are utterly irrelevant to their core function, existing as a separate layer of human construction.

For the chimp, a banana is far more than just a piece of fruit; it is concentrated energy, vital sustenance, and a valuable social currency that can reinforce dominance, appease a rival, or forge a fleeting alliance. For humans, however, the "banana" has diversified into myriad forms, constantly evolving and abstracting with our increasing societal complexity:

The most tangible are material bananas. These encompass money, property, vast tracts of land, critical natural resources like oil, gas, rare earth minerals, or fresh water, and the endless array of luxury goods that signify status and comfort. The relentless pursuit of wealth, the drive to accumulate vast fortunes, the fierce competition for fertile ground or valuable mineral deposits—these are all direct manifestations of the primal hoarding instinct, amplified by our economic systems. This explains why billionaires continue to amass billions long past any conceivable personal or even generational need; it's not about necessity, but the sheer, amoral thrill of the acquisition, the expansion of their hoard, and the undeniable power that comes with it.

Beyond the physical, we relentlessly crave social and emotional bananas. We actively pursue attention, validation, admiration, love, loyalty, and a positive reputation. These are vital for social

4

cohesion, influence within a group, and personal well-being. A social media influencer chasing "likes" and "shares" is, in essence, seeking social bananas, transforming fleeting digital affirmation into a form of influence. A person meticulously curating their public image for widespread admiration is engaged in a sophisticated form of reputation acquisition, hoping to leverage perceived virtue for tangible benefits. Even the seemingly altruistic desire for a romantic partner, while often cloaked in sentiment and affection, is fundamentally driven by the pursuit of emotional and reproductive bananas—companionship, genetic propagation, shared resources, and the comfort of mutual support.

Then there are the highly sought-after power and control bananas. These include formal authority, decision-making capabilities that affect multitudes, the ability to influence or outright control the actions of others, and perhaps most fundamentally, the freedom from external control or coercion. Political office, corporate leadership, or even simply being the dominant voice within a family or friendship group—these are all highly coveted forms of power bananas, granting unparalleled access to further resources and influence. The innate drive to lead, to govern, to command, is a direct and unmistakable echo of the chimp's primal quest for alpha status, albeit expressed through the incredibly intricate and often veiled systems of human governance.

In the modern age, particularly in our information-saturated society, informational bananas have become incredibly potent. Knowledge, secrets, strategic insights, proprietary intellectual property, and data itself—these are invaluable currencies. In a world increasingly shaped by the flow and control of information, possessing key data is a profound form of leverage, a banana that can be swiftly converted into material wealth, social influence, or crucial strategic advantage over competitors. The pervasive espionage activities of nations, the relentless data harvesting of tech corporations, the global race for scientific breakthroughs and patented discoveries—all are sophisticated quests for informational bananas, recognizing that information is power, and power secures more.

And finally, perhaps the most abstract, yet deeply compelling, are existential bananas. Our relentless human pursuit of meaning, purpose, or a sense of belonging can be viewed as the acquisition of psychological stability, a way to mitigate the inherent anxieties of an indifferent universe. Whether through fervent religious faith, a steadfast philosophical conviction, or unwavering dedication to a grand cause, we seek narratives and structures that provide comfort, coherence, and a perceived place in the cosmic order, offering a vital form of psychological resource that allows us to function and thrive.

Our sophisticated human brains, far from eliminating these primal drives, merely equip us with an unparalleled toolkit to achieve them. Where a chimp might rely on raw brute strength to dominate a rival or snatch a desired item, we construct intricate legal contracts, orchestrate complex global financial schemes, launch persuasive marketing campaigns that subtly shape desires, or engage in the nuanced manipulation of social dynamics. The elegance of human "banana stealing" lies in its indirection, its profound subtlety, and its almost boundless capacity for elaborate justification. We don't always directly snatch; we often create incredibly complex systems—economic, social, political—where the banana is effectively funnelled to us, all while meticulously maintaining an illusion of fairness, merit, or even moral righteousness. We bestow lofty names upon these processes, calling them lobbying, negotiation, innovation, strategic partnership, or simply "working hard," while the fundamental amoral imperative remains unchanged: acquire the banana.

This book will serve as your unflinching guide through this often uncomfortable reality, systematically dismantling the layers of illusion to expose the raw machinery beneath. We'll delve into the biological imperatives that hardwire us, exploring the "Sentinel's Gaze" that compels us to constantly scan our environment for threats and opportunities, and the fundamental "Dominance Drive" that relentlessly compels us to seek hierarchy and control. We'll expose the societal constructs that humanity has so painstakingly invented, the "Narrative Veils" of ideologies, laws, religions, and cultural myths, all ingeniously designed to disguise our true nature and justify our amoral pursuits, creating the illusion of inherent goodness. We'll trace these timeless dynamics through "The Human Story in Action," from ancient conflicts like the archetypal "Original Banana War" to the strategic brilliance and insidious nature of "The Fine Art of the Trap" in both historical and modern contexts. We'll then zoom in on the specific battlefields of our Modern Banana Wars, dissecting the political arena as a grand stage for power struggles, the insatiable pursuit of wealth as the "Ultimate Hoard," and the ruthless "Unwritten Rule" of "Finders Keepers, Losers Weepers" that governs all competition, from corporations to individuals. Finally, in "The Mirror and the Future," we'll confront any lingering illusions head-on, addressing apparent counter-arguments like the "Bonobo Paradox" by re-framing cooperation itself as merely a strategic tool for collective self-interest. We'll then project the "Echoes of Ape-oca-lypse," exploring the profound and often grim implications of what happens when our powerful amoral drives are truly unleashed on a global, technologically advanced scale. Ultimately, we will challenge you, the reader, to consider what it truly means to be "Living Without Illusions," embracing this raw reality not for despair, but for personal effectiveness and strategic navigation in a world that operates on principles far older and colder than any moral code.

Be warned: this isn't a feel-good journey, nor is it intended to provide comforting platitudes. The truth, in its purest form, rarely is. You might squirm, experiencing a deep-seated discomfort as long-held beliefs are challenged. You might resist, feeling a profound psychological urge to defend the cherished notion of inherent human goodness and altruism. You might even find yourself arguing back against these very pages, as if a comfortable, indispensable illusion is being violently stripped away. But if you dare to truly listen and hear—without the need for a metaphorical "flapper" hitting you on the ear to distract you from inconvenient truths—you'll gain an unflinching understanding of humanity, and of yourself, that is simultaneously profoundly unsettling and remarkably liberating. Because once you truly see the banana for what it is—a prize of survival and propagation—and the chimp who relentlessly pursues it, you can't unsee them. And you'll realize, with unsettling clarity and perhaps a wry, knowing smile, that this means you.

Chapter Two
The Great Illusion: Why We Invent Morality

We tell ourselves stories. From the earliest flickering camp-fires illuminating the fearful darkness to the sprawling, interconnected narratives of our modern digital age, we spin intricate tales of heroism and villainy, of selfless sacrifice and wicked betrayal. We meticulously teach our children from their first conscious moments about right and wrong, about fairness and compassion, about the imperative to share and the inherent virtue of kindness. We instinctively recoil from and publicly punish the cruel, effusively praise the kind, and tirelessly strive to live by a complex, often contradictory, code that we fundamentally believe distinguishes us from the "beasts" from which we supposedly ascended. This intricate code, this unwavering internal compass we clutch so tightly, guiding us through perceived realms of good and evil, fairness and justice, we proudly call morality.

It is, without question, humanity's most cherished and enduring illusion, a grand spectacle of self-deception that has allowed us to build civilizations while simultaneously masking the raw, amoral drives that power every brick and beam. This illusion is not merely a quaint belief; it's the very bedrock of our self-perception, the comforting narrative that allows us to sleep at night convinced of our own elevated nature, a stark contrast to the relentless, unblinking pursuit of "bananas" that truly defines our species. The sheer persistence of this illusion, its pervasiveness across cultures, religions, and eras, speaks to its profound utility. It's not a mistake of cognition, but a deliberate, albeit subconscious, evolutionary strategy, honed over countless generations. We embrace it because it allows us to reconcile our self-serving actions with a desire for social harmony, to participate in collective endeavors without confronting the uncomfortable truth of our own underlying motivations. It's the ultimate psychological lubricant, smoothing the rough edges of our primal urges so that we can function in complex social structures without constant, overt conflict.

Because if you strip away the comforting layers of cultural conditioning, the rigid dictates of religious dogma that promise divine reward or eternal damnation, and the lofty, often impenetrable, abstractions of philosophical treatises, you will find that "morality" is not some inherent force of the universe, a divine imperative whispered from on high, or even a universal truth etched immutably into the helix of our very DNA. It is, instead, a brilliant, highly adaptive, and utterly convenient fiction. This fiction, meticulously woven into the very fabric of our societies since time immemorial, serves as an ingenious mechanism for managing the intricate, often brutal, dynamics of the banana game, the relentless pursuit of resources, power, and status that we explored in the preceding chapter. It provides a deceptively elegant framework for fostering group cohesion, an artful justification for our deep-seated self-interest, and a powerfully effective tool for subtly controlling the actions of others within the collective, all while maintaining the veneer of higher purpose. The invention of morality allowed nascent human communities to move beyond brute-force hierarchies, enabling the formation of larger, more complex groups that could cooperate on an unprecedented scale. It codified expectations, established norms for resource distribution, and laid the groundwork for complex legal systems, all of which ultimately served the amoral goal of survival and prosperity for the group and its individuals.

Consider what we so readily label "good." An act of charity, for instance, might appear, on the surface, to be the purest expression of selflessness, a genuine giving without expectation of return. Envision a wealthy individual donating a vast sum to a distant cause, perhaps funding a school in a developing nation, or a dedicated volunteer tirelessly dedicating countless hours to helping complete strangers in a faraway land, asking for nothing in return. From the conventional perspective, these are actions of unadulterated benevolence, shining examples of humanity's capacity for universal love. Yet, dig deeper, beyond the immediate appearance and the laudable outcome, and the motivations often become far more nuanced, even when profound societal benefits are achieved. Is the charity driven, perhaps, by a shrewd desire for social status, public acclaim, or the prestigious awards, accolades, and tax breaks that often follow such magnanimous gestures? Could it be a subconscious attempt to alleviate an internal sense of guilt or to assuage the profound discomfort of witnessing suffering that might otherwise disturb one's carefully constructed peace of mind? Does it serve to gain invaluable access to influential networks, powerful individuals, or future business opportunities, where a reputation for benevolence demonstrably opens doors and fosters trust? Might it even be a strategic maneuver to secure reciprocal help in the future, establishing unspoken credits in a social bank account that can be drawn upon later in times of personal or collective need? Or, more subtly still, could it simply be a means to "feel good" about oneself, a powerful intrinsic psychological reward system where the brain floods with neurochemicals like dopamine and oxytocin, reinforcing the behavior through a pleasurable feedback loop that ensures its repetition? Could it be a calculated move to reinforce a group's cohesion against an outside threat, subtly painting the "givers" as virtuous and superior, and the "takers" as needing guidance or even subjugation, thereby strengthening internal bonds and subtly justifying exclusion or dominance over others within or outside the tribe? While the outcome of such an act may indeed be profoundly beneficial to others, the motivation, viewed through the cold, amoral lens, almost invariably traces back to a complex, multi-layered form of self-interest, however subtle, psychologically intricate, or socially ingrained its pathways. This doesn't negate the tangible benefit of the act itself, but it fundamentally redefines the driving force, stripping away the illusion of pure altruism and revealing the evolutionary calculus beneath. The very definition of "good" becomes a highly flexible and context-dependent tool for communal and individual advantage.

And what of "evil"? When we vehemently condemn an act as evil—be it a brutal crime that shocks our collective sensibilities, a tyrannical regime that systematically subjugates a populace, or a blatant act of betrayal that shatters the very foundations of trust within a community—are we truly judging it against some cosmic scale of absolute right and wrong, an objective measure of universal malevolence handed down from a divine authority? Or are we, more accurately and more fundamentally, reacting to a direct or indirect violation of our personal "banana security," our deeply ingrained tribal norms, or our carefully constructed social hierarchies? The "villain" in our grand narratives is, at their core, simply the chimp who steals our banana, or who attempts to steal or operate in a way that fundamentally disrupts our preferred social order, often to their own overwhelming advantage, threatening our established flow of resources. Their "evil" is not defined by some inherent universal wickedness, a black mark on their soul, but by the tangible threat they pose to our access to vital resources, our cherished status within the group, or our fundamental safety and comfort. Consider the historical "evils" of colonialism, often justified by the colonizers as bringing "civilization" or "salvation" to "primitive" peoples, while simultaneously seizing their land, resources, and labor for the benefit of the conquering power. Or the "evil" of heresy, swiftly and brutally punished by religious institutions not out of cosmic moral rectitude, but to maintain doctrinal purity and, by extension, their own absolute power and control over their flock and the narratives that sustain them. History, in its unvarnished telling, is replete with chilling examples where what one group ferociously labels "evil" is viewed by another as a necessary, strategic, or even virtuous act of self-preservation, rightful conquest, or divine will. The condemnation of "evil" is less about objective morality and more about the perceived detrimental impact on one's own acquisition or retention of bananas, a powerful emotional and social tool wielded to rally communal resistance against a perceived threat and justify its suppression. It's a pragmatic defense mechanism, not a universal judgment.

This stark realization is not to suggest that laws are useless, or that compassion isn't a powerful and observable force in human interaction. Quite the contrary. These constructs—our intricate legal codes, our profound expressions of empathy, our deeply held societal values—are incredibly sophisticated and highly effective tools. They are, in essence, the advanced rulebooks for the human banana game, designed not by some benevolent universal consciousness, but forged in the crucible of evolutionary necessity. Laws establish boundaries, creating predictability and minimizing internal conflict that would otherwise drain resources from the primary goal of external competition and resource acquisition. Compassion, far from being purely selfless, can be a highly adaptive mechanism for fostering reciprocity, strengthening group bonds, and ensuring that valuable genetic material (kin) or productive allies are preserved. These seemingly "moral" behaviors are the result of countless generations of natural selection, favoring individuals and groups that developed mechanisms for cooperation and self-regulation over those that succumbed to internal chaos. But it is to assert that the underlying reason for their existence, their ultimate "why," is not an adherence to some external, immutable moral absolute. Instead, these intricate dualistic constructs of right and wrong, justice and injustice, order and chaos, emerge organically from the messy, relentless, and unceasing pursuit of survival, propagation, and advantage – for the individual, for the tightly knit family unit, for the broader tribe, or even, in those rare moments of collective insight, for the species as a whole. What we call "morality" is simply the most efficient, most adaptable, and most effective set of rules, behaviors, and shared narratives that has allowed specific groups of chimps (us) to acquire and protect their bananas in a given environment, at a given time, thereby ensuring their continued existence and often their dominance over other groups. It is a brilliant social technology, refined over millennia, that helps large groups of inherently self-interested individuals cooperate just enough to outcompete other groups, to more efficiently exploit their environment, and to ultimately secure a greater share of the world's limited bananas for themselves. Without this shared "fiction," the sheer scale of human cooperation, from building cities to launching rockets, from establishing complex trade networks to fighting global pandemics, would simply be impossible, as unbridled individual self-interest would invariably lead to chaotic dissolution. The illusion of morality provides the necessary framework for this fragile, yet immensely powerful, cooperation.

This truth, when first confronted, can be utterly terrifying. It relentlessly strips away the comforting belief in an inherent, universal goodness that underpins so much of our self-perception and societal structure. It dismantles the reassuring notion that there's a grand, benevolent design guiding our actions or justly judging our transgressions from afar. It forces us to acknowledge a deeper, colder, and far more primal reality that often clashes with our romanticized view of ourselves. This realization can feel like an emotional earthquake, shaking the very foundations of how we've been taught to see ourselves and the world. It can feel like a betrayal, a loss of something sacred. But, paradoxically, it is also profoundly liberating. It frees us from the impossible, often crippling, burden of perpetually striving to live up to a phantom ideal, an elusive moral perfection that simply does not exist in the biological realm. This profound clarity allows us to see human behavior—including our own—with chilling precision and a dispassionate analytical gaze: as the calculated, adaptive strategies of the most successful, most cunning banana-stealers on the planet, driven by forces far older and more powerful than any moral code we might invent or profess. It allows us to analyze interactions, anticipate behaviors, and navigate the intricate, often ruthless, dance of human society not through a fog of idealistic assumptions, but with the sharp, unblinking clarity of pragmatic realism. This clarity offers not cynicism, but a powerful new lens through which to truly understand the human condition, empowering us to make more effective choices based on reality, rather than illusion. It is the ability to play the game with full knowledge of its rules, rather than clinging to a rulebook that never truly existed.

Chapter Three

The Flappers and the Blind: Why Humanity Refuses to Hear the Truth

The Flappers and the Blind: Why Humanity Refuses to Hear the Truth

If the truth of our amoral nature is so self-evident, as the relentless pursuit of resources implies, then why don't we simply acknowledge it? Why do we recoil? Why do we persist in constructing elaborate facades of morality and altruism? The answer, ironically, can be found among Swift's strange inhabitants of a floating island: the Laputans.

These peculiar people, residing in the abstract heavens of mathematics and music, were so engrossed in their lofty calculations and theoretical musings that they often failed to perceive the very world around them. To function, they required servants, "flappers," to gently strike them with bladders filled with peas or pebbles – on the mouth to prompt speech, and on the ear to command attention. Without this constant physical jolt, they drifted through life, oblivious to dangers, opportunities, or even simple conversations.

We are, in many ways, the Laputans of our own existence. Humanity, especially its intellectual elite and its system architects, too often lives on a metaphorical floating island of abstract concepts: complex economic theories, intricate political ideologies, and sophisticated moral philosophies. We become so engrossed in the elegance of our systems, the purity of our ideals, or the perceived correctness of our beliefs that we simply fail to "hear" the messy, amoral reality unfolding beneath our feet. We dismiss the constant, grubby scramble for advantages as an unfortunate anomaly, a deviation from the "true" path, rather than the fundamental engine of our species. This blindness, however, isn't solely intellectual detachment; it's a profound, often unconscious, resistance rooted deeply in our cognitive architecture and evolutionary history. To truly accept our amoral nature – meaning a fundamental lack of an inherent moral compass rather than a predisposition to evil or malevolence – is to shed comforting illusions: the belief in inherent goodness, the promise of universal justice, and the notion that our species is on a linear path toward moral perfection. It's a terrifying prospect, a stripping away of the narratives that give many lives meaning and cohesion, revealing a more complex, self-serving, yet undeniably human core.

Our minds are not dispassionate observers; they are highly efficient, albeit often biased, information processors that frequently prioritize mental comfort and self-preservation over stark reality. One powerful tool in this cognitive toolkit is Confirmation Bias, which wires us to seek out, interpret, and remember information that confirms our pre-existing beliefs, particularly those that flatter our self-perception and group identity. When faced with evidence of relentless self-interest—the "grubby scramble" for resources—we filter it out, rationalize it as an exception, or reinterpret it through a moral lens. Consider how often media narratives frame geopolitical conflicts purely as battles between good and evil, conveniently overlooking the underlying scramble for strategic advantage, economic dominance, or vital resources. Similarly, an individual deeply committed to a particular political ideology will readily absorb news that praises their party's actions as principled while dismissing identical actions by opponents as corrupt, further entrenching their comfortable illusion. We want to believe in the righteous cause, making it harder to acknowledge the amoral drivers. Coupled with this is Self-Serving Bias and the Fundamental Attribution Error, where we readily attribute our own gains and questionable decisions to external circumstances or necessity ("I had no choice," "everyone else does it"). Conversely, we attribute others' similar actions to their inherent flaws, greed, or immorality. A business leader might justify aggressive market tactics, such as hostile takeovers or mass layoffs, as "smart strategy" and "necessary restructuring" to ensure shareholder value, while condemning a competitor's identical actions as "unethical exploitation." This psychological sleight of hand protects our self-image and perpetuates the illusion of our own (and our group's) moral superiority. The way information is presented, known as Framing Effects, also profoundly influences our acceptance; frame a policy as a "moral duty" or "social justice imperative," and it garners support far more readily than if it's presented as a pragmatic reallocation of resources based on power dynamics. For instance, a carbon tax might be presented as a "moral imperative to save the planet" rather than a mechanism to shift economic burden and generate revenue, making it more palatable. We simply prefer the moral wrapper, even if the underlying content is purely about who gains what. Furthermore, Optimism Bias and Illusory Superiority lead most people to genuinely believe they are more ethical, more intelligent, and less susceptible to primitive impulses than the average person. This pervasive sense of illusory superiority makes it difficult to recognize the amoral currents that drive everyone, ourselves included; it's the silent conviction that "I'm not one of those who would steal a banana, not really," even as we maximize our own gains. Finally, the Sunk Cost Fallacy reveals our reluctance to abandon a deeply invested belief system—be it a personal code of conduct, a national ideology, or a religious doctrine—even in the face of contradictory evidence. The emotional and intellectual "cost" of admitting that our foundational beliefs (like inherent human goodness or a linear path to moral perfection) might be false can be too high to bear. For example, a nation might persist in an unpopular war, framing it as a "fight for freedom," long after its material objectives have become clear and its moral justifications have eroded, simply because admitting the true cost and amoral drivers would invalidate years of sacrifice and political capital. We double down on the illusion rather than accept the painful truth.

Beyond these cognitive blinders, our capacity for self-deception and our comfort with moral narratives aren't random glitches; they may be deeply ingrained evolutionary adaptations. From an evolutionary perspective, the belief in morality, even if an illusion, served a powerful adaptive function as a "Social Glue" for group cohesion. A shared narrative of "good" and "bad," enforced through rituals, taboos, and stories, facilitated cooperation, punished defectors, and allowed for the formation of larger, more complex societies. This system, for instance, encourages reciprocal altruism, where individuals help others with the expectation of future returns, a form of "moral" behavior that ultimately serves self-interest. Acts of apparent self-sacrifice, like a parent protecting their child or a soldier defending comrades, can often be understood through the lens of kin selection or group survival—maximizing the propagation of shared genes or securing the survival of one's interdependent unit. What might appear as unconditional love or selfless devotion can often be rooted in these deeply ingrained, evolutionarily advantageous mechanisms. Groups that could collectively agree on a "moral" framework for resource distribution and behavior might have outcompeted those that couldn't, allowing for more effective collective "banana gathering" (i.e., resource acquisition), even if individual motivations remained amoral. What appears to be pure altruism often functions as an "Honest Signal" of status, trustworthiness, or future reciprocal benefit; individuals perceived as "moral" gain social capital, which can translate into greater access to resources, mates, or allies. For instance, a wealthy individual making a large charitable donation gains public esteem and influence, which may bring future opportunities or simply reinforce their social position. Our brains might have evolved to find moral narratives comforting precisely because they facilitated social survival and individual advancement. Believing in one's own "goodness" also makes one a more convincing deceiver, a better player in the social game of acquiring benefits, as genuinely believing your own lies makes them more believable to others. Moreover, neuroscientists and evolutionary psychologists suggest that a degree of self-deception, acting as a "Blind Spot Mechanism," can be beneficial by reducing anxiety, increasing confidence, and allowing us to pursue goals with fewer debilitating doubts. This allows for bolder, more decisive action in competitive environments without the internal conflict that true self-awareness might bring, a practical advantage in the ongoing struggle for resources. It's crucial to understand that identifying these adaptive underpinnings of behavior is not to reduce human experience to crude biological determinism, but rather to reveal the deep-seated tendencies upon which our complex social structures and self-conceptions are built.

This refusal to acknowledge our amoral core is not unique to any single culture or era; it is a universal human trait, manifesting in diverse forms across the globe and throughout history. The Laputans are everywhere. Every human society, regardless of its specific values, constructs elaborate systems of "morality" that serve, at least in part, to obscure or justify the underlying amoral drivers of resource acquisition and power. All major Religious Systems provide comprehensive moral codes, dictating right and wrong, yet a dispassionate look reveals how these codes have historically been leveraged to justify conflict, conquest, and the systematic acquisition of resources. Consider the Spanish Conquistadors, who, driven by an insatiable hunger for gold and land, justified their brutal subjugation of indigenous populations with the "moral imperative" of converting them to Christianity, demonstrating how spiritual zeal can be a powerful veneer for material gain. The "will of God" often conveniently aligns with the interests of the powerful. Even sophisticated Philosophical Traditions, intended for rational inquiry, can become their own "floating islands." Think of how grand political philosophies, from communism to extreme libertarianism, often describe an ideal, rational human actor or a perfectly just society, while overlooking the messy, often contradictory, self-interested behaviors of individuals in practice. Philosophers like John Locke, with his theories of natural rights and a societal contract based on reason, or Karl Marx, with his vision of a classless society free from exploitation, offered profound insights into societal structures. Yet, their blueprints for moral or just societies often struggled in practice to account for the relentless pull of self-interest, group interest, and raw power dynamics that derail their utopian ideals. They became so engrossed in the purity of their theoretical constructs that the messy reality of human motivation was dismissed as an imperfection, rather than the fundamental engine. Furthermore, it's a romantic illusion to view Indigenous Cultures as purely harmonious and untouched by the "banana wars." While their moral frameworks often emphasize reciprocity and communal well-being within the tribe, historical and anthropological records reveal internal conflicts, resource competition, and narratives justifying actions against rival tribes for territory, hunting grounds, or captives. The very act of defining an "in-group" and "out-group" establishes a subtle moral boundary, where reciprocal obligations and "good" behavior often cease at the tribal frontier, illustrating the same underlying amoral imperative for group survival and prosperity.

The form of the moral facade may differ across cultures, but the function of obscuring amoral drives remains consistent. In Collectivist Societies, the "good" is frequently defined by group harmony, conformity, and duty, which can beautifully mask individual self-interest operating within those structures, where personal

gain is pursued through status within the collective or by enhancing the collective's competitive edge. For instance, an individual
might work tirelessly for the "glory of the nation," participating
in state-sponsored enterprises, but their underlying motivation
might include personal advancement within the party, securing a
comfortable life through state resources, or ensuring the security
of their family unit. In contrast, Individualist Societies use concepts
like "freedom," "rights," and "meritocracy" as moral veneers for intense competitive accumulation, where the "right" to pursue one's
own "bananas" is paramount, even if it leads to vast inequalities.
The narrative of "pulling yourself up by your bootstraps" morally
justifies extreme wealth disparities as the natural outcome of individual effort and freedom, obscuring the systemic advantages and
disadvantages that shape resource distribution and often blaming
victims for their lack of "moral" fortitude or effort. In Honor/Shame
Cultures, the pursuit of "honor," which often translates to social
dominance, reputation, and control over resources, is cloaked
in moral imperative; dishonor is a profound threat not just to
personal dignity, but to one's ability to secure benefits and protect
social standing. Disputes over perceived slights, for example, can
escalate into violent conflicts justified as upholding family or tribal
honor, when at their core they are about asserting dominance
and control over social and material capital. Lastly, many cultures
operate on a system of "Polite Fictions"—societal agreements to
uphold certain agreeable falsehoods or convenient omissions to
maintain social order. Everyone implicitly understands the underlying truth, but to speak it aloud would be disruptive; this is the
subtle societal "flapper" that prevents uncomfortable truths about
power and self-interest from being openly discussed. Consider
how, in many social settings, people avoid direct confrontation or
criticism, even when fully aware of underlying issues, to maintain a
façade of harmony, which serves to preserve the existing social hierarchy and power dynamics without challenging uncomfortable
truths.

Fortunately, various academic disciplines, sometimes unwittingly, serve as our "flappers," offering insights that challenge our comfortable illusions and reveal the underlying amoral drivers. Economics, despite its occasional oversimplifications, provides tools like Rational Choice Theory which fundamentally presumes self-interest as the primary motivator, aligning with our core premise of maximizing individual or group gains. The classic economic model of a perfectly rational actor relentlessly pursuing self-interest, though often criticized for its lack of real-world applicability, ironically provides a clear, unvarnished view of human motivation. Behavioral Economics delves deeper, studying how our cognitive biases, emotions, and psychological quirks lead to what might seem like "irrational" economic decisions but are, from our perspective, predictable manifestations of our deep-seated amoral pursuit of gain. It shows how seemingly irrational choices, such as impulse buying or aversion to loss, stem from deeper, often non-conscious, drives of acquiring or protecting resources. Furthermore, Resource Scarcity & Conflict Theory directly links competition over vital resources to conflict, regardless of ideological or moral justifications, from historical land grabs to modern water wars. In Political Science and International Relations, the school of Realism/Neo-Realism posits that states act primarily out of self-interest, driven by power and security in an anarchic world. Moral arguments are often seen as post-hoc justifications or cynical tools to legitimize power grabs; for instance, a "humanitarian intervention" is frequently examined through the lens of strategic interests, such as securing access to natural resources or establishing regional influence, rather than purely altruistic motives. The constant, relentless struggle for control over resources, people, and narratives is the true engine of Power Dynamics in politics, where rhetoric about "justice" or "democracy" often serves as a morally palatable disguise. Likewise, Propaganda & Rhetoric systematically use moral language to manipulate populations, justify inequalities, and legitimize the acquisition of resources, as seen in wartime narratives that demonize the enemy while glorifying one's own nation's cause. Moving to Sociology and Anthropology, while Social Constructionism acknowledges that morality's specific forms are human constructs, our argument is that the underlying drivers of resource acquisition and dominance are not; the forms may vary, but their function of masking amoral drives remains constant. Social norms, laws, and institutions, while appearing to enforce morality, ultimately regulate how gains (resources, status, opportunities) are distributed within a society. Cultural Relativism similarly highlights that while moral rules differ, their purpose—to regulate resource distribution and maintain social order for the benefit of some—is universal. Symbolic Interactionism shows how shared symbols and meanings like "justice" create a social reality that can obscure raw power dynamics, leading people to internalize societal expectations that, on closer inspection, often serve existing power structures. Finally, Neuroscience provides a physiological basis for this denial. Our brains are hardwired for immediate gratification and reward through Reward Systems, with dopamine circuits driving us towards acquiring perceived benefits, often overriding long-term "moral" considerations or abstract principles. While Empathy is a powerful human trait, neuroscience shows it is often limited to in-groups—we are more likely to feel empathy for "our" tribe's gains than another's losses—and can be selectively switched off or overridden when resource competition or perceived threat is high, or when moral justification allows for dehumanization. Similarly, Confirmation Bias has a neural basis, with our brains actively processing information to reinforce existing beliefs, effectively "tuning out" contradictory signals and maintaining our moral illusions. These varied academic lenses collectively deliver the precise, targeted tap of the flapper, revealing how deeply ingrained our denial truly is.

Despite the overwhelming evidence from every corner of human inquiry, the self-imposed deafness persists for powerful reasons. The "flapper's tap" is painful because it threatens the very foundations of our perceived reality and identity. There's the pervasive Existential Dread that arises if humanity is not inherently good, if progress isn't a march towards moral perfection, or if universal justice is a comforting fiction. This realization can trigger profound existential anxiety, stripping away the narratives that give many lives meaning and purpose. To realize that life is an amoral scramble for resources can feel like standing naked in a cosmic void, questioning the very purpose of existence if not for a higher moral aim. There's also the perceived threat of Social Disintegration—a deep-seated fear that if the "moral illusion" crumbles, society itself will descend into chaos. This fear, however, often confuses the descriptive (what is) with the prescriptive (what should be); the belief that acknowledging a truth will automatically cause its negative manifestation. But historical examples, from the French Revolution to various tribal conflicts, show that chaos often arises from unacknowledged power struggles and resource grabs, rather than the cessation of moral belief. Indeed, a clear-eyed view of human nature might lead to more robust, rather than fragile, social contracts. Furthermore, accepting an amoral reality can trigger a Personal Identity Crisis for individuals who have built their lives around strong moral principles, whether they are religious leaders, passionate activists, or simply those striving to be "good citizens." Their entire edifice of self-worth and life choices may feel challenged, implying that their core motivations, even if seemingly altruistic, might be rooted in something far more primal, self-interested, or evolutionarily adaptive than they care to admit. Finally, acknowledging the amoral reality forces us to confront our own Complicity; we are all, to varying degrees, participants, beneficiaries, or victims of the ongoing competition for resources. This can be deeply uncomfortable, as it removes the comforting distinction between "good" people (we) and "bad" people (they), revealing a more complex, less flattering truth about humanity. We are all, at some level, chimpanzees vying for our share of gains.

This book, then, intends to be your flapper. It is designed to deliver that sharp, necessary tap to your perception, to make you listen to what our biology, our history, and our daily observations relentlessly scream. It's time to step off the floating island of comforting fiction and confront the amoral reality below.

To accept the amoral nature of humanity is not a descent into nihilism or an endorsement of cruelty. Quite the opposite. It is the beginning of clear-eyed realism. It is the necessary prerequisite for genuinely understanding human behavior, for building more robust and effective societal structures, and for navigating the relentless pursuit of advantages with a strategic mind rather than a deluded heart. Only when we fully comprehend the true drivers of human action can we construct truly resilient systems, not based on utopian moral ideals, but on the pragmatic reality of our species. This understanding empowers us to design systems that anticipate and manage the human drive for gain, rather than being perpetually surprised by its manifestations. It allows for a more nuanced approach to conflict resolution, resource allocation, and even personal interactions, seeing the underlying game clearly.

Like Swift's Laputans, we have the capacity to drift endlessly in our abstract, self-referential heavens, oblivious to the dangers and opportunities unfolding beneath us. We can cling to our elegant theories and pristine ideals, waiting for a "moral awakening" that will never come, because the very premise of inherent morality is a phantom. Or we can choose to feel the sharp, liberating tap of reality. The flapper's blunt instrument is not meant to harm, but to awaken. It is a reminder that the world is messy, driven by forces we'd rather not acknowledge, but which nevertheless dictate much of our existence. Only by truly hearing that tap—by acknowledging the undeniable, unceasing, and fundamentally amoral scramble for resources that defines our species—can we finally step off our intellectual floating island and engage with the world as it truly is, rather than as we wish it to be. The choice to listen, or remain blissfully blind, is now yours. This choice determines whether we continue our contented drift, destined to be surprised by every bump and jolt, or whether we awaken to the true mechanisms of human behavior, prepared to navigate the turbulent currents of our amoral reality with open eyes.

Chapter Four

The Narrative Veil: How We Weave Stories to Justify the Steal

Having peered through the illusion of inherent morality in the preceding chapter and having felt the uncomfortable tap of the flapper reminding us of our own persistent blindness, we must now confront the apex of human ingenuity: the very mechanism that sustains this grand deception. Chimps, as we've established, simply take bananas. Their motivations are raw, direct, and transparent in their primal efficiency. They don't convene solemn conferences afterward to debate the ethical implications of their actions, nor do they compose elaborate manifestos explaining why their particular grab was a selfless service to the troop or a necessary act for jungle stability. Humans, however, do precisely that. We don't just steal; we meticulously spin the steal. We cloak our raw, amoral pursuits—our fundamental drives for survival, propagation, and acquisition—in elaborate, often breathtakingly beautiful, narratives, creating a pervasive and intricate "veil" so deeply woven into the fabric of our perception that we often entirely forget what unvarnished reality lies beneath. This narrative veil is not merely a polite cover-up; it is humanity's most sophisticated tool, far more potent and effective than any stone axe, cunning trap, or even the most advanced digital algorithm. It's the unparalleled art of transforming bald self-interest into universal truth, naked dominance into sacred duty, and brutal acquisition into unquestionable justice, thereby making the most egregious banana grabs not only palatable but often celebrated.

This "narrative veil" functions as a kind of collective cognitive dissonance amplifier, allowing entire societies to operate on principles that contradict their underlying drivers. It is the mechanism by which individuals rationalize their own actions, and by which groups justify their dominance over others. The power of this veil stems from its ability to appeal to our higher cognitive functions—our craving for meaning, for order, for belonging—while simultaneously serving the baser, amoral instincts. It's the ultimate bait-and-switch: promising moral elevation while facilitating material gain. Indeed, the very capacity for this complex self-deception appears to have been a crucial evolutionary advantage for our species. Early human groups that could forge shared myths and beliefs, even if those beliefs were convenient fictions about shared purpose or moral righteousness, were able to cooperate on a scale unprecedented in the animal kingdom. This collective cohesion, built on a foundation of shared, albeit fabricated, narratives, allowed them to outcompete other hominid groups, to hunt larger prey, to defend territory more effectively, and to distribute resources (bananas) more efficiently within their own ranks. The ability to believe in the same story, regardless of its objective truth, cemented bonds and enabled complex social structures to emerge, granting a decisive edge in the brutal game of survival and propagation. The narrative veil wasn't an accidental byproduct of consciousness; it was a fundamental driver of our ascent.

Consider, for example, the sheer, transformative power of language and euphemism as fundamental threads in this veil. We rarely describe our aggressive pursuits or their unpleasant consequences with direct, unvarnished terms. Instead, wars, those brutal, bloody struggles for resources, territory, or geopolitical dominance, become sanitized as "operations," "interventions," or noble "peacekeeping missions," even when peace is the furthest outcome. The true cost of human lives, shattered societies, and environmental devastation is submerged beneath clinical terms like "collateral damage" (human lives) or "pacification" (subjugation by force). Corporate layoffs, those deliberate sacrifices of thousands of livelihoods for increased profit margins or shareholder value, are rebranded as "restructuring," "downsizing," "right-sizing," or "optimizing human capital," transforming painful human displacement into an abstract, almost benign, business necessity. Financial crises, the predictable outcomes of systemic greed, reckless speculation, and unchecked power consolidation, are explained away as "market corrections," "unforeseen circumstances," or the enigmatic "invisible hand" at work, absolving individuals of responsibility. We invent entire vocabularies specifically designed to disinfect our actions, to make the banana grab palatable, even laudable, by removing its sharp edges and its direct moral implications. This linguistic alchemy allows us to speak of immense suffering and ruthless acquisition in abstract, detached terms, maintaining a comfortable psychological distance from the visceral reality of human impact. It's a psychological buffer, enabling us to act ruthlessly without feeling truly ruthless, ensuring our internal narrative of "goodness" remains intact.

Beyond mere words, our very laws and justice systems, often held up as the pinnacle of human moral progress and the definitive proof of our elevated consciousness, are fundamentally integral parts of this narrative veil. They are not expressions of objective, universal right and wrong handed down from some cosmic arbiter. Instead, they are, in essence, meticulously codified rules designed primarily to protect the "bananas" of the dominant group that crafted them. These laws dictate precisely how bananas are to be divided, who is allowed to steal from whom within the permissible framework (e.g., through taxation or corporate mergers), and what constitutes a "legitimate" grab versus

an illegal one. "Justice" in this context often means the maintenance of an established order that demonstrably benefits those
who constructed and currently control the laws, with punishments
serving as powerful deterrents against any actions that threaten
the existing distribution of resources and power. Think of the
historical evolution of property laws: they didn't emerge from a
universal moral imperative but from the need to secure the assets
of a land-owning or merchant class. From the enclosure acts that
privatized communal lands, dispossessing vast populations for
agricultural efficiency, to modern intellectual property rights that
lock down knowledge for corporate gain, preventing widespread
access, laws create a legitimate framework for inherently amoral
acquisition, ensuring the powerful continue to hoard their gains
while maintaining the illusion of fairness and impartiality. The
sheer scale of the legal apparatus and its accompanying narrative
of impartiality lend immense authority to these rules, making
them appear absolute and righteous rather than pragmatic tools
of control.

Then there are the grand constructs of ideologies—political,
economic, and social. These are colossal narratives that provide compelling "moral" justifications for how societies should be
structured, how power should be exercised, and how resources
should flow. Capitalism presents itself as the path to individual
freedom and prosperity, morally superior because it supposedly
rewards merit and hard work, while simultaneously facilitating the
concentration of immense wealth and power in the hands of a
few through competitive acquisition and often exploitative labor
practices. Communism promised ultimate equality and collective
good, justifying revolutionary violence and totalitarian control in
the name of a future utopia, all while consolidating state power
and resources under an elite few. Democracy champions individual rights and self-determination, yet its mechanisms can be
subtly manipulated through campaign finance, gerrymandering,
and media control to ensure that the "banana distribution" re-

mains largely undisturbed for entrenched interests. Fascism, with its emphasis on national purity and strength, morally justifies aggression, ethnic cleansing, and conquest as necessary for the survival and glory of the chosen people, enabling brutal expansionism for territorial and resource acquisition. None of these are objective truths; they are incredibly compelling stories that effectively mobilize vast populations, rationalize otherwise horrific actions, and ultimately facilitate specific forms of "banana acquisition" and control for particular groups, be they economic classes, racial groups, or national entities. They provide the shared delusion necessary for collective amoral action on a truly massive scale, inspiring loyalty, sacrifice, and even death in the name of a fabricated higher purpose.

Perhaps the oldest, deepest, and most enduring thread in this intricate narrative veil is religion. For millennia, sacred texts, ancient myths, and complex doctrines have provided divine sanction for humanity's most primal and amoral actions. Conquest becomes a "holy war," a divine mandate to claim a promised land, rather than a brutal invasion for territory and resources. Inequality—the stark reality of some having vastly more bananas than others—is explained away as God's will, karmic destiny, or a test of faith, conveniently alleviating the powerful of any moral responsibility for the plight of the weak and ensuring the continuation of their privilege. Religious commandments, while appearing to promote "good" behaviors like honesty and kindness, often primarily serve to establish social order, control populations, and ensure the perpetuation and dominance of the specific group that interprets and enforces them – all fundamental forms of "banana protection" and acquisition within a given social system. The promise of an afterlife or spiritual salvation becomes a powerful motivator, subtly diverting attention from earthly injustices and encouraging compliance with the existing order, effectively making the dispossessed accept their lot in exchange for a future, unseen banana. Religious leaders, often among the most successful banana-acquirers, wield immense influence by controlling the very definition of "good" and "evil" for their followers, thereby directing their behaviors and loyalties.

And nowhere is this narrative veil more intensely, deliberately, and chillingly woven than within the confined, suffocating ecosystems of cults. Here, a charismatic leader, often deeply disturbed yet profoundly adept at psychological manipulation, constructs an entirely new reality, a bespoke moral universe explicitly designed for their followers. Doctrines within a cult are crafted with surgical precision to justify the leader's absolute power, the members' extreme sacrifices (often including wealth, family, personal autonomy, and even life itself), and their forced isolation from the "evil" or "unenlightened" outside world. The "morality" within a cult is entirely self-referential and circular, serving only the leader's insatiable acquisition of wealth, sexual access, and psychological control over every aspect of their followers' lives. Members are persuaded that their complete surrender to the cult's dogma and the leader's will is the highest moral act, a path to ultimate salvation, enlightenment, a guarantee of a better reincarnation or a utopian future, while in truth, it's often their ultimate dispossession – of identity, resources, agency, and often, their very lives. The cult leader, the master weaver of this specific veil, exemplifies the amoral imperative stripped of all societal pretense, showcasing how readily individuals will surrender their "bananas" when a compelling enough false narrative is provided.

This narrative veil doesn't merely hide our amoral nature; it actively facilitates its grandest, most ambitious expressions. By creating shared fictions—shared beliefs in justice, divine mandates, economic fairness, or collective salvation—humanity enables cooperation on scales utterly unimaginable for mere chimps, who are limited by direct observation and immediate reciprocity. This collective self-deception allows us to orchestrate "banana steals" of entire continents, to manipulate global economies for the benefit of a select few, and even to subtly control the aspirations and lives of billions, all while confidently proclaiming our moral supe-riority and noble intentions. This is the ultimate human paradox: our greatest capacity for collective action, for building complex civilizations and achieving monumental feats, is often powered by our greatest capacity for profound and pervasive self-deception. It is the lie we tell ourselves that allows us to thrive, to conquer, and to hoard, convincing ourselves that our amoral pursuit is, in fact, the most moral path.

However, despite its immense utility, relying solely on this nar-rative veil carries an inherent cost and vulnerability. When reality diverges too sharply from comforting fiction, the veil can become a liability. Collective self-deception, while enabling cooperation, can simultaneously blind us to impending crises, foster irrational decisions based on distorted perceptions, and hinder effective problem-solving. Consider societies that clung to outdated eco-nomic ideologies in the face of mounting evidence, or political systems that denied existential threats until it was too late. The very strength of the narrative veil—its ability to create shared belief—can become its weakness, leading to groupthink and a conformity bias where dissent is suppressed and uncomfortable truths are actively avoided. Individuals, driven by a deep-seated need for cognitive closure and a psychological desire to belong, will often engage in motivated reasoning, selectively interpret-ing data to fit the existing narrative, even when confronted with contradictory evidence. This preference for coherence over truth, while emotionally reassuring, can lead entire populations down disastrous paths, making them unable to adapt to genuine threats or exploit genuine opportunities because their perception of re-ality has been irrevocably warped by the very fictions designed to protect them. The narrative veil, while making us powerful banana-acquirers, also renders us susceptible to the dangers that come from seeing only what we wish to see. Our ultimate chal-lenge, therefore, lies in learning to navigate the world with the clear sight that comes from pulling back this veil, even if only for a moment, to understand the true, amoral forces that propel us all.

Chapter Five

The Sentinel's Gaze: Hardwired for Enemies (and Opportunities)

W e've relentlessly stripped away the comforting illusions of
inherent morality, exposing them as sophisticated human
fictions. We've endured the uncomfortable tap of the flapper,
reminding us of our own persistent blindness to the self-serving
nature hidden beneath our noble narratives. Now, with a clearer
vision, it's time to dig deeper still, beneath the intricate layers of
culture and language, beyond the constructs of society, into the
very bedrock of our biology. We must travel back, far back, to
the unforgiving, sun-baked plains and dense woodlands where
humanity first emerged from the primordial soup of pre-hominid
existence. For it is there, in the relentless crucible of survival,
where life and death hung in a delicate, hourly balance, that the
primary lens through which we view the world, the fundamental
mechanism for assessing reality, was forged and indelibly etched
into our very being.

Imagine our ancestors, small, vulnerable bands of hominids,
navigating the treacherous African savanna. Life was not a leisure-
ly stroll through an open-air museum; it was a relentless, visceral
dance between predator and prey, a constant oscillation between
dire scarcity and fleeting opportunity. Every rustle in the tall grass,

barely discernible, carried the potential for an immediate, existential threat—a lurking lion, a venomous snake, or a rival tribe encroaching on precious territory. Every fleeting shadow on the distant horizon, every unfamiliar face encountered at a scarce waterhole, carried the potential for immediate, fatal peril. Those who survived this brutal lottery, those whose genes successfully propagated into the future, were not contemplative philosophers or the empathetic dreamers. They were the ones exquisitely tuned to danger, the ones whose very nervous systems had been honed to an unparalleled degree of vigilance. They possessed an inherent, automatic sentinel's gaze – a hyper-vigilant, subconscious scanning of the entire environment, not for beauty or abstract contemplation, but for anything that might kill them, or, crucially, anything that might feed them and their kin.

This wasn't a conscious choice, a learned behavior, or a philosophical inclination; it was a biological imperative, as fundamental as breathing. Our brains, particularly the ancient, reptilian and limbic structures, evolved specifically to prioritize threat detection above all else. A suspicious glance from a stranger, a sudden, unexpected movement in the periphery of vision, an unfamiliar scent carried on the wind – these were not cues for polite conversation or philosophical debate. They were instantaneous triggers for an immediate, life-saving fight, flight, or freeze response. The very survival of the individual, and by extension, the precious gene pool, depended entirely on this constant, often subconscious, split-second assessment of friend versus foe, safety versus peril. The cost of a false positive (seeing a threat where none existed) was minimal – a wasted burst of adrenaline. The cost of a false negative (failing to see a real threat) was absolute – immediate death. Natural selection relentlessly favored the paranoid, the vigilant, the quick to react. It wired us for suspicion, for fear, and for immediate action, long before we developed the capacity for complex moral reasoning. This sentinel's gaze, therefore, operates entirely outside the realm of morality; it is purely a mechanism of self-preservation, ensuring the continuity of the organism and its genetic lineage.

But here's the critical, often overlooked, and profoundly illuminating twist: the very same neural pathways and instinctual mechanisms that perfected our ancestors' ability to spot a mortal enemy also honed their equally crucial capacity to identify an opportunity. The weak gazelle, separated from its protective herd, represented not just a potential danger if ignored, but a banana ripe for the taking, a chance for vital sustenance. The distant smoke from a rival tribe's fire signified not just an encroaching danger, but potentially abandoned resources, a vulnerable camp, or an opportunity to seize a new, more fertile territory. Even the scowl or subtle shift in posture on a fellow group member's face wasn't just a sign of anger or internal conflict, but a crucial signal of a potential challenge, an opening to assert dominance, to climb the internal hierarchy, and thereby secure a larger, more favorable share of the group's spoils. This dual function of the sentinel's gaze – spotting both imminent threat and fleeting opportunity – laid the absolute foundation for the most fundamental and pervasive division in human existence: we versus they.

"We" became the small, familiar band: those with whom one could share the dangers of the hunt, cooperate for mutual defense against external threats, and rely on for reciprocal "banana sharing" within the group. These were the individuals whose faces, gestures, and intentions were known, predictable, and thus, deemed "safe" enough for limited trust. This inherent drive manifests as in-group favoritism, a deeply ingrained bias where we automatically attribute positive qualities, trustworthiness, and shared values to members of our own group, even when based on arbitrary distinctions. Conversely, "they" became everyone else: the distant tribes, the unknown faces, the potential competitors for scarce resources, the implicit threats to the family unit, or the outright obstacles to expansion and prosperity. This wasn't a moral judgment in the classical sense, not an assessment of inherent "goodness" or "evil." It was a cold, pragmatic calculation for survival, driven by the amoral imperative. Our ancestors didn't perceive abstract "evil" in the rival tribe; they perceived competitors for the same fertile hunting grounds, the same precious water holes, the same advantageous caves, the same desirable mating opportunities. Their very existence threatened our banana supply, and therefore, they were a threat to be eliminated or avoided, not a moral equal to be reasoned with. This automatic classification of others as rivals or threats is known as out-group derogation, and it ensures that the "we" group, bound by this existential necessity, reinforces its cooperative unit essential for collective banana acquisition and defense by viewing outsiders with suspicion or hostility.

This ancient wiring, forged in the relentless heat of the savanna, is still deeply and irrevocably embedded within us, despite our modern veneer of civilization and sophistication. It's why we form quick, often unconscious, judgments about strangers based on superficial cues. It's why tribalism arises so naturally and powerfully in seemingly disparate arenas like sports teams, national politics, social causes, and even consumer brand loyalties. Our brains continue to categorize, to divide, to identify "us" and "them" with alarming speed and conviction, a process often dramatically amplified by the perceived scarcity of resources or the exaggeration of threat. In times of real or imagined limited "bananas"—be it jobs, status, or cultural influence—the sentinel's gaze sharpens, and the "we versus they" dynamic intensifies, often leading to xenophobia, protectionism, or conflict. This mechanism is expertly exploited in modern contexts: political campaigns create existential threats (e.g., immigrants, rival ideologies) to mobilize their base, and economic narratives of limited resources are used to justify hoarding or aggressive competition.

In the political arena, this translates into the automatic demonization of opposing parties, where "their" policies are not merely different, but actively "evil" or "dangerous" to "our" way of life, even when common ground objectively exists. The rhetoric of "us vs. them" becomes a powerful tool for political leaders to secure their "political bananas"—votes, power, control—by mobilizing their base against a perceived external threat, often one that is manufactured or grossly exaggerated. In business and economics, the sentinel's gaze manifests as cutthroat competition in markets, where rival companies are not just competitors but adversaries whose failure is desired. Mergers and acquisitions are often described in terms of "conquering territory" or "eliminating threats," direct echoes of primal resource grabs. Employer-employee dynamics, global trade negotiations, and even individual career advancement are all subtle expressions of this constant scanning for advantage, for the opportunity to secure a larger portion of the societal banana. Our modern media environment, particularly social media, has become a potent amplifier for this ancient wiring, creating echo chambers that reinforce in-group narratives and constantly highlight out-group "threats," triggering our sentinel's gaze on an unprecedented scale and often leading to rapid polarization and the spread of misinformation. Consumerism itself leverages this: advertising often taps into a primal desire for status and belonging (in-group) by presenting products as essential for joining a desirable "tribe" or differentiating oneself from others (out-group).

This primal instinct extends beyond grand societal interactions, permeating our most intimate social dynamics. Consider the subtle dance within a social group: who gains influence, whose opinions hold sway, who controls the flow of information and attention – these are mini-banana games. The sentinel's gaze subconsciously assesses new acquaintances not just for friendship, but for their potential utility or threat. It analyzes conversations for openings to assert status, subtly undermine rivals, or gain an advantage. This innate wiring explains why we derive such deep, visceral satisfaction not just from our own side winning, but often from the opposing side losing—their "banana" diminished, their status reduced, our "banana" thereby secured and our dominance reinforced. This schadenfreude, far from being a moral failing, is a deep-seated biological reward, a testament to the fact that resource scarcity and competition are still etched into our very reward systems. The sentinel's gaze, honed in the brutal classrooms of the savanna, continues to scan, not just for the physical lion in the grass, but for the weakness in our competitor's argument, the leverage in a negotiation, the momentary lapse in attention from which to snatch a quick gain, or the profound opportunity to secure our next big bite of the banana, always measuring the risk and reward for us.

Significantly, this deep-seated, ancient wiring operates largely at a subconscious level, often overriding our more recently evolved rational thought processes. We can intellectualize about universal brotherhood and ethical principles, but when the alarm bells of the sentinel's gaze go off—perceiving a threat to our resources, status, or group identity—the primal response often takes over, coloring our perceptions and directing our actions. This makes it incredibly difficult to intellectually bypass or simply reason away this primal wiring. Even with explicit knowledge of these biases, our brains remain susceptible to motivated reasoning, selectively interpreting evidence to support pre-existing beliefs that align with our group identity or perceived self-interest. This deeply in-grained conformity bias also ensures that individuals often align their perceptions with the group, even against their own better judgment, to maintain social harmony and avoid the threat of out-group status within their own "we." It is the default setting of our operating system, constantly running in the background, shaping our perceptions and subtly directing our behavior. The challenge of consciously overriding this ancient programming highlights the immense power of the amoral imperative; under-standing these forces is the first step, as simply "knowing" isn't enough to counteract millennia of evolutionary programming. To truly understand human behavior, then, requires acknowledging

41

this fundamental, amoral lens through which we constantly filter reality. It is the first, most powerful layer of our inherent being that must be understood to truly navigate the banana game effectively, to recognize when we are acting on ancient impulse rather than rational choice, and to strategically leverage this primal understanding in our interactions, rather than being blindly driven by it.

Chapter Six

The Dominance Drive:

Hormones, Hierarchy, and

the Quest for the Top

Banana

The Immutable Engine: The Primal Dominance Drive

We've peeled back the layers of comforting illusions surrounding morality and exposed the intricate narrative veils we instinctively weave to obscure our amoral drives. But merely identifying these illusions and deceptions is insufficient; we must now confront the deeper, pulsating current that animates them. Having understood how our ancestors' sentinel gaze honed their ability to spot both danger and opportunity, the profound question remains: what primal, unyielding force compels them, and by extension, us, to relentlessly seize and act on those opportunities, irrespective of learned societal norms or abstract ethical codes? What ignites the ceaseless scramble for advantage, for control, for that coveted "top banana" in every conceivable human endeavor?

The answer lies not in learned behavior, not in abstract philosophy, nor even solely in cultural conditioning. Instead, it is embedded deep within the immutable bedrock of our biology: a powerful, ancient, and insatiable engine known as the dominance drive.

This drive is fueled by a potent, fluctuating cocktail of hormones and neurochemicals that dictate our very place in the intricate, often brutal, pecking order of existence. This drive is not a societal construct to be debated or chosen; it is a fundamental, inherited imperative, sculpted by millennia of relentless evolutionary pressure, ensuring the most effective individuals and groups rise to secure the lion's share of resources and reproductive success. It is the unvarnished, amoral engine of existence.

To grasp the visceral, unvarnished reality of this drive, one need only observe a chimpanzee troop in its natural habitat. It is anything but a free-for-all, a chaotic jumble of individuals. Instead, it is a meticulously structured, rigidly defined society, held together by an often-brutal, yet paradoxically stable, hierarchy. At the apex sits the undisputed alpha male, the magnificent "top chimp," his broad shoulders radiating an undeniable aura of authority. He is the first to feed, claiming the choicest morsels; he enjoys prime access to all fertile females; and he commands the safest, most comfortable resting spots. But his elevated position isn't simply about brute strength, though that remains a foundational element. His dominance is a precarious throne, constantly maintained through a complex, high-stakes interplay of subtle intimidation (a fixed stare, a puffed-up gait), strategic alliances with loyal, ambitious subordinates who hope to one day inherit his mantle, and frequent, assertive displays of raw power (charging, drumming, aggressive vocalizations) that reinforce his authority. Perhaps most fascinatingly, the alpha often performs a surprising degree of "justice" or mediation within the troop, breaking up fights among lower-ranking members. This isn't altruism; it's a shrewd, pragmatic maneuver to prevent excessive internal strife that could weaken the troop against external threats, thereby serving to maintain the alpha's own stability, his unchallenged access to vital resources, and the overall cohesion that benefits his genetic lineage. This relentless quest for the alpha position, and the fierce, vigilant defense of it once attained, is not a deviation from their nature; it is the fundamental, existential purpose of their lives, dictating resource flow, reproductive success, and the very survival of the lineage. Every interaction, every glance, every grooming session in the troop is, at its core, a subtle negotiation and reaffirmation of this profound power dynamic.

Humans, despite our self-proclaimed intellectual superiority and our sophisticated cultural trappings, operate by a remarkably similar, albeit vastly more nuanced and intellectually elaborate, biological script. Our own lives are pervasively defined by hierarchies, from the seemingly trivial (who leads a casual conversation or gains the most likes on a social media post) to the profoundly significant. Consider the relentless ascent of the corporate ladder, where individuals sacrifice personal life and endure immense stress for a sliver of added authority; the cutthroat, no-holds-barred competition for political power, where the stakes can involve controlling the fate of nations; the subtle but undeniable establishment of social standing within a friend group, dictating who influences decisions or gains attention; or the grand geopolitical struggle for global influence, resources, and ideological supremacy. This constant, often subconscious, striving for position, for status, for the upper hand in every interaction, isn't merely learned behavior picked up from cultural norms, though culture undoubtedly shapes its expression. Instead, it's deeply ingrained, an innate impulse driven by the very chemicals coursing through our veins. It's a biological program that rewards the climb with profound internal satisfaction and penalizes the fall with deep discomfort, relentlessly pushing individuals and groups to secure preferential access to "bananas" in all their myriad forms, from tangible wealth to intangible respect. The forms of dominance may change—from physical might to intellectual prowess, from accumulated wealth to fleeting celebrity, from moral authority to sheer manipulative skill—and indeed, the acceptable expressions and even the intensity of this drive vary significantly across cultures and historical periods. But the underlying drive remains constant, pushing individuals and groups to incessantly seek a higher rung on the societal ladder.

This fundamental drive is orchestrated by a complex interplay of neurochemical signals, meticulously refined by evolution to optimize survival and reproduction. While reconstructing the precise evolutionary path of these mechanisms is complex, their fundamental role in driving status-seeking behavior is observable in both human physiology and comparative animal studies today. It is important to note that these neurochemicals operate within an incredibly complex and dynamic biological system, and our focus here is on their established, prominent roles in mediating dominance-related behaviors.

Consider the profound and pervasive role of testosterone, often simplistically stereotyped merely as the "male" hormone. While more prominent in males, it plays a critical, albeit context-dependent, role in both sexes in driving competitive behavior, assertiveness, risk-taking, and status-seeking. Higher baseline testosterone levels are frequently associated with a heightened drive to win and an increased likelihood of initiating or responding to challenges to one's position. It primes the individual for confrontation and for seizing opportunities, often increasing a person's physical and mental readiness for competition. Intriguingly, research reveals a powerful "winner effect": a victory, whether in a sporting event, a business negotiation, or a political debate, can cause a subsequent surge in testosterone, further increasing confidence, risk-taking, and the drive to seek out future contests. This creates a potent positive feedback loop, literally hardening the resolve of the victor and encouraging further pursuit of dominance, thereby reinforcing the underlying neurobiology and shaping brain circuitry over time. Conversely, low testosterone can be associated with submissive behaviors and a reduced drive to compete.

Fluctuations in cortisol, the primary stress hormone, are intimately tied to challenges to one's status or the profound, debilitating anxiety of maintaining it. A chimp losing a physical fight for dominance, or a human facing a public defeat in a debate, a career setback, or a devastating social humiliation, will often experience a rapid, agonizing surge in cortisol, signaling the physiological cost of their lowered position or threatened status. This biochemical response not only registers the immediate stress but also serves as a potent internal feedback mechanism, driving the individual to avoid similar losses in the future or to redouble desperate efforts to regain lost standing. The crushing, unpleasant sensation associated with low status relentlessly reinforces the drive to avoid it, at almost any cost, and can lead to chronic stress, vigilance, and even immunosuppression in subordinate individuals. Like testosterone, these cortisol responses also feed back, influencing the brain's processing of future social cues and shaping behavioral responses to hierarchy.

Then there's serotonin, often simplistically associated with mood and happiness. In many social species, including primates and, profoundly, our own, serotonin levels correlate significantly with an individual's place in the hierarchy. Those with higher, more stable status frequently exhibit higher, more stable serotonin levels, which are associated with feelings of well-being, confidence, reduced anxiety, and a greater sense of calm authority. This neurochemical stability contributes to the "aura" of command and self-assurance often seen in effective leaders, making them appear more capable and less rattled. Conversely, individuals lower down the hierarchical ladder may experience the inverse, with lower serotonin levels contributing to feelings of anxiety, heightened vigilance (a constant, unrewarded sentinel's gaze), chronic stress, submission, or even clinical depression. This isn't just a side effect of status; it's a powerful biological incentive system, meticulously crafted by evolution. It rewards the arduous climb up the hierarchy with neurochemical pleasure and psychological resilience, and it penalizes the fall or prolonged low status with physiological discomfort and diminished mood, thereby relentlessly pushing individuals to continually seek a higher position or maintain the one they have, ensuring a constant churning and fierce competition for status within any social group. Furthermore, while the dominance drive is genetically encoded, its precise expression can be further fine-tuned by epigenetic modifications, where environmental experiences, particularly early in development, influence how these underlying biological programs are 'read' and translated into behavior.

But perhaps the most powerful and addictive neurochemical component of the dominance drive is dopamine. Often referred to as the "reward" chemical, dopamine is not just about pleasure after an achievement; it's more powerfully associated with the anticipation of reward and the drive to seek it. The very thought of gaining a higher position, achieving a victory, or securing a coveted "banana" triggers a dopamine rush, motivating the individual to pursue that goal with intense focus and persistence. When the "banana" is finally acquired, another dopamine surge provides a fleeting sense of satisfaction, immediately followed by a subtle craving for the next one, perpetuating the cycle. This creates a powerful positive feedback loop, a neurochemical addiction to the climb itself, making the relentless quest for dominance an inherently self-perpetuating, insatiable desire. It is the engine of motivation, constantly pushing for more, better, faster, higher.

The "quest for the top banana" is, therefore, far more than merely symbolic; it is a fundamental, biologically engineered imperative, driven by this intricate symphony of hormones and neurotransmitters. For our ancestors, and still for us, higher dominance translated directly and unequivocally into tangible "bananas" – resources that directly impacted survival and reproductive success in the most visceral ways: Resource Access: This was paramount. The dominant individual or group secured better access to vital food sources, prime hunting grounds, safer shelters, and more reliable water holes. In modern terms, this translates to preferential access to vast wealth, prime real estate, exclusive opportunities, critical information, influential networks, and strategic assets, all of which confer immense power and comfort. From an economic perspective, this directly impacts capital accumulation and distribution. Mating Opportunities and Reproductive Success: For any species, the ultimate amoral imperative is to pass on one's genes. Higher dominance directly correlated with increased access to the most desirable mates, ensuring greater reproductive success, the propagation of one's genetic lineage, and a greater number of offspring with a higher likelihood of survival. This remains a powerful, often unspoken, motivator in human social and sexual dynamics, manifesting in attraction to success, power, and prestige. This is a core tenet of evolutionary psychology and sociobiology. Influence and Control: The dominant individual or group gained the ability not just to direct the collective, but to shape its very reality, to make decisions that primarily benefited themselves and their immediate kin or allies, and to secure unwavering loyalty and obedience from subordinates through a mix of fear and perceived benefit. This translates into political power, unchallenged leadership roles, and the ability to dictate policies, cultural norms, and economic systems in one's favor, ensuring a continuous flow of bananas. This touches upon political science, sociology, and anthropology. Reduced Vulnerability and Increased Security: Being at the top minimized the likelihood of being challenged, exploited, or displaced by rivals. It conferred a degree of safety, predictability, and insulation from consequence, allowing the dominant entity to conserve precious energy and resources that lower-ranked individuals had to expend constantly on vigilance, defense, and appeasement. This manifests today as security, privilege, immunity from certain laws, and the ability to take greater risks with less personal fallout. In criminology and legal studies, this explains disparities in enforcement and consequence. Psychological Well-being and Cognitive Function: The neurochemical rewards associated with dominance—the dopamine hits, the stable serotonin, the confident testosterone—translate into a profound, often unconscious, sense of well-being, control, and purpose. This intrinsic reward is a powerful motivator in itself, making the climb inherently satisfying, regardless of external validation. Conversely, chronic low status can lead to diminished cognitive function and increased susceptibility to mental health issues, a critical area of study in neuroscience and psychology. The drive isn't just for external gain, but for internal neurochemical homeostasis.

This profound, biologically rooted dominance drive is the silent, pervasive force behind countless human interactions, whether we acknowledge it or not. It operates in every arena, from the grand geopolitical stage where nations vie for global supremacy and resource control, to the most intimate personal relationships, where individuals subtly jockey for emotional or decision-making power. Whether it's the CEO fighting fiercely for market share and corporate growth, driven by an insatiable desire to crush competitors; the politician vying relentlessly for votes and legislative control, knowing that power is the ultimate banana; the social media influencer chasing likes, followers, and lucrative brand deals to secure digital status and economic gain; the academic striving for tenure and recognition; or even the subtle power plays within a family unit – these are all direct, albeit culturally modulated and often disguised, manifestations of the same ancient dominance drive. While dominance manifests in many forms, some individuals exhibit personality traits that particularly amplify their effectiveness in the relentless pursuit of status, leveraging psychological strategies that are highly adaptive for securing control.

It's crucial to distinguish this biological imperative from morality. This drive is not about being "good" or "evil" in a moral sense; such concepts are irrelevant to its operation. It's about being effective, about securing advantage, about the relentless, biologically mandated pursuit of more: more resources, more control, more influence, more security. It's about the inherent, amoral drive to ascend the hierarchy and secure unimpeded access to the sweetest, most abundant "bananas," and crucially, to deny them to rivals, thereby ensuring one's own survival and perpetuation. Understanding this immutable engine is not an absolution of responsibility, but rather a crucial first step towards intelligently navigating and channeling its powerful currents within human societies. Our elaborate social structures, our complex economic systems, even our moral narratives are, in essence, sophisticated extensions of this primal biological engine, brilliantly designed to manage, channel, and often exploit the relentless human quest for the top. The constant striving, the ceaseless competition, the innate desire to win—these aren't learned vices, but fundamental, unshakeable expressions of our biological heritage, ensuring that the "banana game" is played with an intensity that only nature could engineer.

Chapter Seven

The Original Banana War: Cain, Abel, and the Genesis of Conflict

Humanity's remarkable ascent to planetary dominance isn't a testament to innate virtue, but rather a chillingly effective application of our "cognitive toolkit," amplifying an amoral imperative for raw acquisition – a truth vividly explored in "The Naked Ape's Toolkit: From Stone to Strategy." Building upon the foundational insights of Desmond Morris's seminal "The Naked Ape," which similarly aimed to strip away the veneer of human sophistication to reveal our primate core, this treatise sharpens its focus on humanity's distinct "toolkit" – both tangible and cognitive – as the true, amplifying engine behind our species' unparalleled success and dominance. While Morris famously highlighted our biological nakedness, this work delves into how our unique capacity for elaborate tool-making and sophisticated strategy became the ultimate mechanism for fulfilling our inherent amoral imperative, pushing us far beyond mere instinct into unprecedented levels of acquisition. The preceding chapters, which have explored the biological wiring of the sentinel's gaze perpetually scanning for threats and opportunities, and the ceaseless, insatiable drive for dominance pushing us relentlessly up every conceivable hierarchy, lay the groundwork for understanding how these primal impulses manifest in subtle social cues, corporate battles, and even the very architecture of our brains, acting as silent, amoral directors of our most fundamental behaviors. This current chapter then asks how these foundational, amoral forces translate into the grand narratives that have profoundly shaped human history, the very stories we tell ourselves about who we are, why we fight, and what we believe. It investigates how the raw, unvarnished biological imperatives become transmuted into the moralistic tales that define our cultural consciousness. To truly understand this intricate process of self-deception and collective myth-making, the chapter turns to perhaps the most ancient and potently resonant tale of human conflict, one that has echoed through millennia, shaping moral thought and religious doctrine, yet whose true, chillingly pragmatic, amoral core remains stubbornly, brilliantly obscured: the story of Cain and Abel. This foundational myth, often misinterpreted through a purely moralistic lens, holds within its stark simplicity the brutal, pragmatic truth of humanity's competitive ascent, laying bare the raw mechanics of "banana-stealing" at the dawn of civilization, providing a timeless lens through which to examine all subsequent human strife.

The familiar narrative paints a clear, almost universally accepted, picture of good versus evil: two brothers, children of the first human pair, Adam and Eve, each bringing an offering to God. One offering, Abel's, a shepherd's sacrifice of the "firstborn of his flock and of their fat portions," is accepted by divine favor, the smoke of his burnt offering rising pleasingly to the heavens. The other, Cain's, a farmer's offering of "fruit of the ground," is pointedly, conspicuously rejected, leaving his countenance fallen and his spirit consumed by bitterness. Jealousy, a cardinal sin and often cited as the root of this tragedy, festers in Cain's heart, leading to a profound "moral transgression"—the ultimate act of fratricide—and finally, a just divine punishment that casts him out from his family and the fertile land. It's a story we hold up as a foundational lesson in sin, envy, the catastrophic consequences of moral failure, and the immutable distinction between right-eousness and wickedness. It is presented as a bedrock principle for understanding human depravity and the necessity of divine law, a timeless warning against the dangers of covetousness and unbridled rage. Indeed, countless sermons, theological treatises, philosophical discourses, and works of art have been built upon this interpretation across diverse cultures and epochs, cementing it as an archetypal allegory for the eternal struggle between good and evil, with Cain as the embodiment of humanity's dark poten-tial and Abel as the innocent victim of malevolence. This moral framework serves to neatly categorize human actions, providing a sense of order and accountability in a world often defined by chaos.

But let us, for a moment, strip away the intricate, multi-layered veil of morality and theological interpretation that has cloaked this story for millennia. Let us see this primordial drama not through the stained-glass lens of sin and divine judgment, nor the comforting shroud of moral absolutes, but through the cold, unadulterated, biologically informed lens of pure, unabashed ba-nana-stealing. When viewed this way, the story transforms from a simple moral parable into a chillingly accurate blueprint for all subsequent human conflict, a microcosm of the amoral impera-tive at work, revealing the deep-seated drives that continue to fuel our competitive nature, long after the theological dressings have been applied. This reframing allows us to bypass the prescriptive judgments of right and wrong and instead analyze the underly-ing, universal forces that compel action, revealing a pattern that repeats in every struggle for advantage. What, then, were the "bananas" truly at stake for Cain and Abel in this foundational sibling rivalry? Not merely the literal produce of their labor – a few sheep or some harvested grain, though these were certainly valuable commodities in a nascent agricultural society. The stakes were far, far more valuable in the nascent, brutally competitive human world, where status and perceived worth directly translated into survival advantage, access to scarce resources, and the very continuation of one's lineage. The true bananas were divine favor, social validation, and ultimate legitimacy. In a world without complex social structures, where direct access to resources and the perceived backing of a higher power dictated one's place and future prospects, God's acceptance of Abel's offering, and the pointed, public rejection of Cain's, was not merely a spiritual slight. It was a devastatingly public declaration of one brother's higher standing, his greater "worth" in the eyes of the ultimate authority in their limited universe. This act of divine selection implicitly conferred a superior position, a greater share of intangible but immensely valuable "social bananas" privilege, respect, and perhaps even a subtle assurance of future prosperity. For Cain, a diligent farmer whose painstaking efforts yielded less approval, whose hard work was seemingly devalued and deemed insufficient, this wasn't merely a spiritual slight; it was a profound, undeniable blow to his dominance drive, a public demotion in the nascent, primal social hierarchy of the world's first family. His "banana" in other words his status, his sense of being the favored, the successful one, the one implicitly deemed more fit to receive divine blessing and thus, to prosper and pass on his genes—was being effectively, humiliatingly snatched by his younger brother. This blow struck at the very core of his self-preservation and propagation instincts, which are inextricably linked to status, especially in a small, isolated group where resources and genetic legacy are tightly coupled to social standing. It was an attack on his very claim to existence as a superior individual.

Cain's ensuing rage, that legendary "countenance fallen," wasn't just "sinful envy" in the abstract, a moral failing born of ill will. It was the visceral, explosive, biologically wired frustration of a thwarted dominance drive, a primal response to a perceived loss of territory—not physical land, but social and spiritual ground. His anger, festering visibly on his face, was a clear, unambiguous signal of his perceived loss of status, a primal reaction to being outcompeted, and his acute inability to acquire the highly coveted "banana" of divine favor and validation. The neurochemical storm within him would have been potent: a surge of cortisol signaling the profound stress and physiological cost of his lowered position and the threat to his self-perception; perhaps a precipitous dip in serotonin contributing to feelings of distress, agitation, and a desperate sense of powerlessness; and a thwarted dopamine response that denied him the anticipated reward of success, instead turning his internal reward system into an engine of desperate craving for re-establishment of status and the restoration of his perceived worth. From this amoral, biological perspective, the ultimate, horrifyingly effective solution to this existential threat to his position, to this public diminishment of his "banana" share, was chillingly simple: eliminate the source of his perceived displacement. Killing Abel was the most brutal, yet in a raw, amoral sense, the most utterly efficient and effective method to remove the competition, to reclaim the potential for that singular "top banana" in the family unit, and to ensure his own survival and continued access to resources without rivalry. The act, while horrific, set an early, indelible precedent for the amoral efficiency that would characterize so much of human conflict: identify the obstacle, remove it, take the prize.

The "curse" that follows Cain, his banishment to a life of restless wandering from the fertile land, isn't necessarily a moral judgment from a just God, as tradition often dictates, a punishment for his sin. Instead, it can be seen as the pragmatic, self-regulating mechanism of an emerging social order, a desperate measure taken by a nascent human society for its very survival. For a small, vulnerable human population, clinging precariously to existence, unbridled inter-group violence—even when occurring within the confines of the earliest family unit—was a direct, existential threat to survival and propagation. Such unchecked internal conflict could quickly lead to the annihilation of the entire group, undermining the collective ability to hunt, gather, reproduce, and defend against external threats. Cain's banishment and enforced nomadism can therefore be interpreted as the collective's necessary, amoral response to an individual whose actions jeopardized group cohesion, stability, and the ability to collectively hoard "bananas." His removal was a prophylactic measure, an ancient form of social engineering to prevent the internal disintegration of the tribe before it could even fully form. It was a brutal but logical calculus: the survival of the group outweighs the individual's right to unpunished aggression. The "mark" placed upon Cain is less about eternal damnation and more about a visible sign of consequence, a universally legible warning, not just to Cain, but to any other potential aggressor contemplating similar acts of destabilizing violence. It serves as a necessary social mechanism to identify him as a threat to group harmony, a public deterrent against similar acts, and a means to prevent further internal "banana wars" that would weaken the fragile group. It's the proto-social contract in action, prioritizing the collective's survival (its collective banana of security and prosperity) over the individual's unchecked aggression, establishing a rudimentary form of justice not for moral rectitude, but for group stability and continued resource acquisition. This early societal response, even in its harshness, demonstrates a foundational truth: cooperation, even coerced, often yields more bananas for the group than unfettered individual aggression, a principle that would eventually underpin all laws, governments, and organized societies throughout human history.

The story of Cain and Abel, therefore, resonates with such profound and enduring power not because it primarily teaches us about inherent good and evil in the abstract. Its deep, archetypal resonance stems from the fact that it perfectly encapsulates the timeless, universal, and profoundly amoral struggles that define our species, reflecting them in miniature, offering a condensed version of humanity's enduring conflicts. It is the raw template for sibling rivalry for parental or authority favor, a primal competition for validation, resources, and emotional security, reflective of the dominance drive at its earliest stage, playing out in every family, every boardroom, every political succession, mirroring dynamics observable even in animal behavior, where competition for parental resources, even leading to siblicide in some species, is a harsh evolutionary reality. It is the blueprint for the relentless drive to secure superior access to necessities and to achieve higher social standing, whether expressed through offerings to a deity or through modern economic and social contests, from academic achievement to athletic prowess. It chillingly lays bare the brutal logic of eliminating rivals, the horrifyingly effective, if morally repugnant, strategy of removing competition to ensure one's own unobstructed path to "top banana" status and resource acquisition. This fundamental strategy has been scaled up from a single fratricide to tribal warfare, ethnic cleansing, and industrial-scale genocide throughout human history, where groups identify and eliminate "competitors" for land, resources, or ideological purity, demonstrating a terrifying consistency in human behavior when unconstrained by effective social control. And finally, it illustrates the prioritization of group cohesion (for banana acquisition), showcasing the collective's amoral need to control internal strife to ensure its own survival and prosperity, even if it means sacrificing or exiling an individual. The myth, therefore, isn't just a story about conflict; it's a foundational psychological narrative that helps us process and implicitly accept the brutal realities of our competitive nature, giving them a "moral" framing to make them palatable and understandable within a constructed ethical universe.

This story, transmitted across countless generations, is a foundational myth precisely because it reflects, in miniature, the countless "banana wars" that would follow, escalating in scale and sophistication, but always driven by the same core impulses that played out in the world's very first fratricide. From skirmishes between hunter-gatherer bands over prime hunting grounds, to the organized, state-sponsored wars for territory and resources, to the complex, global geopolitical conflicts for economic dominance and ideological supremacy, the shadow of Cain and Abel stretches across the millennia, a testament to the unchanging nature of our fundamental drives. Early anthropological studies of prehistoric warfare suggest that while violence might have been low in sparse hunter-gatherer societies, the advent of sedentism and agriculture, creating fixed resources and surpluses, often led to increased competition and larger-scale conflict, eerily mirroring the agricultural Cain's grievance over his pastoral brother's perceived advantage. The human story is a ceaseless re-enactment of this primal drama, cloaked in ever more elaborate moral justifications and technological means. The narrative veil, our innate, powerful ability to spin these brutal realities into tales of justice, righteousness, divine will, or national destiny, has allowed us to compartmentalize and rationalize these fundamental amoral acts, enabling us to continue the relentless pursuit of our own "bananas" with a clear, albeit deluded, conscience. Understanding this primal origin, therefore, is not about judging Cain, but about unmasking the enduring, amoral blueprint for conflict that resides within all of us. This myth, in essence, is a cognitive tool in itself—a socially constructed narrative that explains the inexplicable violence of human nature, yet simultaneously legitimizes a deeper, amoral truth: that our most profound conflicts often arise from the raw, unyielding competition for finite resources and supreme status, a competition we are biologically hardwired to relentlessly pursue.

The book seamlessly integrates nuances by explaining how seemingly prosocial behaviors and cooperation function as highly effective cognitive tools within this amoral framework. Capacities like empathy and fairness facilitate large-scale coordination, acting as sophisticated, long-term strategies for collective "banana" acquisition. What appears as altruism, such as resource sharing, is reframed as a strategic investment in group well-being, maximizing individual long-term gains, a concept underscored by evolutionary game theory. Furthermore, the dynamic nature of this toolkit is illuminated by gene-culture co-evolution, where the use of tools created new selective pressures driving further biological and cultural adaptations. This mechanism underscores the continuous evolution of "strategy" as much as "stone." Addressing potential charges of oversimplification, the book carefully defines "amoral" as "not concerned with morality," rather than "immoral," exploring a foundational biological drive that underlies, but doesn't negate, the complex human experience of morality. The "narrative veil" of morality itself is presented as an extraordinarily effective cognitive tool, binding groups and codifying advantageous behaviors. The book's purpose is to understand humanity at its fundamental level, not to justify behavior, arguing that acknowledging these primal drives empowers us to design more effective societal systems, rather than fighting against perceived moral failures. While robust in its argument, it subtly acknowledges the inherent complexities and emergent properties of human societies beyond simple reductionism. The chapter suggests that while it dissects fundamental drives and tools, human behaviors also exhibit complexities not always reducible to simple, linear cause-and-effect relationships, providing intellectual humility without undermining its core premise. Lastly, the pervasive "banana" metaphor is clearly established from the outset as a universal stand-in for any desired resource, from tangible wealth to intangible status. The book's focus remains on identifying these underlying patterns of behavior across history, rather than attempting to catalog every exception. Crucially, the book operates within a scientific, evolutionary, and sociological framework; its analysis of myths like Cain and Abel is intended as a reinterpretation of human behavioral patterns through this lens, not a theological commentary or a refutation of faith or divine truth. The text concludes by noting the "long shadow" cast by this highly effective toolkit. The same tools that ensure prosperity also enable large-scale warfare, exploitation, oppression, and unprecedented environmental degradation. From ancient, flaked stones to modern global finance, the fundamental drive remains the same: an insatiable appetite for "more bananas." This part of our treatise therefore serves as a crucial bridge, explaining how our primal drives are amplified, paving the way for the discussions of historical conflicts, modern power dynamics, and the ultimate consequences of our "amoral truth." Ultimately, the book argues that only by confronting these foundational truths can humanity truly understand its past, navigate its present, and strategically shape its future.

Chapter Eight

Divided We Conquer (Ourselves) : Tribes, Traditions, and Endless Conflict.

Divided We Conquer (Ourselves): Tribes, Traditions, and Endless Conflict.

We have delved deep into the biological wiring that shapes our every interaction: the sentinel's gaze, perpetually scanning the horizon for threats and opportunities, and the ceaseless, insatiable drive for dominance, pushing us relentlessly up every conceivable hierarchy. We have seen how these primal impulses manifest in subtle social cues, corporate battles, and even the very architecture of our brains, acting as silent, amoral directors of our most fundamental behaviors. However, while these individual drives are fundamental, they operate within a crucial, overriding social context: the tribe. For early humans, and indeed for many of our primate relatives, individual survival was inextricably linked to belonging to a group. A solitary chimp is not merely vulnerable; it is a condemned creature, far more susceptible to predators, starvation, and the harsh realities of its environment than one within a supportive, cooperative troop. This inherent, deeply ingrained need for group cohesion, for an identifiable "we" that extends beyond the immediate family unit, is the bedrock upon which all human societies – from the smallest hunter-gatherer bands to the sprawling complexities of modern nation-states – and their inevitable, often bloody, divisions have been built. The very act of seeking out and maintaining this collective "we" is, in itself, a pursuit of a vital "banana": the banana of safety, shared resources, amplified individual power through numbers, and the crucial psychological comfort of belonging, an imperative reinforced by millennia of evolutionary pressure favoring group-oriented behaviors.

Throughout this chapter, "tribe" is employed as an archetypal concept for any self-identifying in-group characterized by shared traditions and distinct from an 'out-group,' irrespective of scale or historical period. While recognizing the complex and often problematic historical and colonial connotations of the term 'tribe' when applied indiscriminately, this framework allows us to analyze the enduring dynamics of group identity, from the earliest human bands to the complex affiliations of modern society, focusing on the fundamental psychological processes rather than specific socio-political structures, and without adhering to a strict anthropological definition in every instance. As small bands of early humans roamed the vast, unpredictable landscapes of the primordial world, adapting to wildly different environments and developing unique survival techniques, distinct tribes began to form spontaneously. Geography, sheer necessity, and the random chance of encounters fostered unique sets of shared experiences that slowly coalesced into rudimentary yet potent traditions, forming the very bedrock of their emergent cultures. These included highly specific hunting methods tailored to local prey, innovative tool-making styles perfected over generations, nuanced communication signals, and, eventually, the subtle yet powerful development of rudimentary forms of ritual, storytelling, and social organization, from shared meals to communal ceremonies. These traditions, initially practical adaptations forged in the crucible of survival, quickly transcended mere utility, as anthropology and sociology reveal. They became powerful, indelible markers of identity – a collective understanding of "this is how we do things, this is what we believe, this is how we survive," creating a self-reinforcing cultural matrix. This nascent, increasingly solidified sense of "we" inevitably and instantly created an implicit, often unspoken "they"—those who did things differently, those who spoke an unfamiliar tongue, those who belonged to other groups and operated under different, perhaps inscrutable, codes. The psychological mechanism of social identity theory began to take root, where an individual's sense of self became inextricably tied to their group membership, enhancing self-esteem through the perceived superiority of their "we" and reinforcing a profound bias towards their collective. This in-group favoritism, often accompanied by an automatic out-group derogation, offered a crucial evolutionary advantage: rapid identification of allies versus potential threats, streamlining survival decisions in a dangerous, uncertain world. Drawing on comparative studies and anthropological data, evolutionary psychology posits that this innate cognitive bias for one's group, coupled with a degree of xenophobia (fear or dislike of strangers), was highly adaptive in ancestral environments where unknown groups represented potential competition for scarce resources or direct physical threats, thus creating powerful predispositions within our collective psyche. While these biases have deep evolutionary roots and biological correlates, it is crucial to recognize that human behavior is remarkably plastic, allowing cultural norms, education, and conscious effort to modulate or even override these primal inclinations in specific contexts.

While the advantages of cooperation within the tribe were undeniably significant – offering amplified efficiency in hunting large game, superior collective defense against both predators and rival human groups, and a vital mechanism for sharing hard-won resources during times of scarcity – the very act of defining and

rior "we" (the colonizers) systematically subjugating a "they" (the indigenous populations) to seize land, labor, and resources—the ultimate massive-scale banana grab, rationalized by self-serving narratives of "civilizing missions" or "divine right" that masked the raw amoral imperative, demonstrating how shared ideology functions as a tool for collective resource acquisition.

Perhaps one of the most intense and revealing modern examples of this tribal dynamic action stripped down to its rawest psychological components is the chilling phenomenon of cults. In a relatively short span of time, often just months or even weeks, a charismatic leader can forge an incredibly powerful and terrifyingly insular "tribe" with its own unique set of "traditions" – often radically different from, and explicitly opposed to, the broader society from which its members are initially drawn. These traditions can include precise language or jargon, idiosyncratic dress codes, stringent dietary restrictions, specific chants and supposed authoritarian teachings, peculiar rituals, and, most critically, a particular and often paranoid worldview that defines the "in-group" as enlightened, chosen, morally superior, or possessing exclusive, ultimate truth. At the same time, the "outside world" is systematically demonized as corrupt, dangerous, ignorant, or even evil. The rapid formation of such intense tribal identity within cults starkly highlights the fundamental human need for belonging and the powerful, almost irresistible influence of shared beliefs and practices, especially when presented by a compelling alpha figure promising ultimate "bananas" like meaning, salvation, guaranteed better next incarnation, or communal safety. The "we vs. they" dynamic is often amplified to an extreme, pathological degree within these groups, with members systematically encouraged (or subtly coerced, and eventually outright forced) to sever all ties with their former "tribes" (family, friends, mainstream society) and to view outsiders with profound suspicion, intense fear, or even outright hostility, often under the explicit direction of the leader who exploits these primal fears to consolidate control and maintain their elevated status within the newly formed hierarchy. This extreme in-group loyalty, coupled with a perceived, often manufactured, threat from the "outside," frequently leads cults to engage in defensive, and sometimes terrifyingly aggressive, behaviors towards the wider world, mirroring the resource competition and threat response that has characterized inter-tribal relations throughout human history. The leader, often acting as the ultimate alpha, dictates the "traditions," controls the flow of information, and relentlessly reinforces the tribal boundaries, ensuring the continued loyalty and absolute control over the group's "bananas"—be it their collective wealth, their labor, their sexual fidelity, or their uncritical non-questioning devotion. These micro-societies illuminate the foundational human propensity to form exclusive groups that consolidate power and resources, mirroring the larger scale dynamics of nations and empires, and serving as stark warnings of how easily these ancient drives can be manipulated. Cult members frequently silo themselves in an echo chamber where only the group's words and edicts bounce back and resonate, reinforcing the leader's authority. In contemporary contexts, such leaders often leverage their control over their group's "bananas" through formalized organizations or businesses, ostensibly offering aid or enlightenment, but in practice consolidating wealth and power through the exploitation of their followers' loyalty and resources, thereby reinforcing their own alpha status within the self-created hierarchy.

Ultimately, the intrinsic human tendency for forming tribes, while initially offering profound survival advantages through co-operation, inherently, and perhaps tragically, sows the seeds of division and inevitable conflict. Our deep-seated need to define ourselves by our shared traditions, beliefs, and practices—our "we"—creates essential psychological boundaries that provide security and identity. Nevertheless, in a world where resources are perceived as finite and perceived threats, both real and imagined, loom large, these self-constructed boundaries all too easily become volatile battle lines. The intense tribalism observed in cults, with its accelerated formation of identity and its stark "we vs. they" mentality, serves as a stark, miniature reminder of this fundamental human dynamic, a chilling microcosm of the larger, often bloody, story of "divided we conquer (ourselves)." "We have met the enemy, and he is us," a sentiment famously encapsulated by Pogo. It underscores that the drive for bananas, amplified by the social construct of the tribe, eternally perpetuates conflict, demonstrating that the very strength derived from our collective identity also contains the inherent weakness of perpetual division. It's important to recognize, however, that these 'we' and 'they' boundaries are rarely static or monolithic; identities can be nested, fluid, and situational, allowing individuals to belong to multiple 'we' groups simultaneously and fostering complex webs of inter-group relationships that transcend simple binary conflict. Many of these groups splinter into subgroups that break away from the original group. This tribal instinct, while a vestige of our evolutionary past, continues to exert a powerful, often subconscious, influence on modern society, manifesting not just in overt conflict but in increasingly polarized political factions, fervent sports fandom, exclusive online echo chambers, and even consumer brand loyalty—all expressions of our fundamental need to belong to a "we" and differentiate from a "they," subtly driving competition for cultural, social, and economic "bananas" even in seemingly peaceful contexts. Recognizing this deep-seated, amoral drive to form exclusive groups and compete against others is crucial for understanding the enduring challenges of achieving genuine global cooperation and shared prosperity, as the primal pull of the tribe often overrides attempts at broader, more universal forms of human solidarity. From a philosophical perspective, it forces us to confront whether our capacity for universal ethics can truly overcome these deeply ingrained, evolutionary, adaptive biases or if such universalism remains a perpetually aspirational, rather than a biologically inherent, state—a question actively debated within the fields of evolutionary ethics and moral philosophy regarding the very foundations and universal applicability of our moral intuitions.

Chapter Nine

The Fine Art of the Trap: From Pitfalls to Predatory Practices.

We've established that the sentinel's gaze spots the banana, an evolutionary adaptation honed for opportunity, and the dominance drives us to instinctively reach for it, propelling us up every conceivable hierarchy. But raw seizure, mere brute force, represents the crudest, most inefficient form of acquisition, often fraught with high risk and limited returns. The truly successful ape, whether a chimpanzee in the rainforest or a human in the concrete jungle, doesn't just snatch; it learns to trap. The fine art of the trap, moving beyond direct confrontation and brute strength, represents a profound evolutionary leap in "banana" acquisition, pivoting from simple brute force to calculated deception, strategic patience, and the sophisticated exploitation of inherent vulnerabilities. This cognitive shift, moving from immediate reactive grab to planned, proactive capture, marks a significant moment in the unfolding of our amoral imperative, highlighting our species' unparalleled capacity for foresight, strategic thinking, and the sophisticated manipulation of both environment and others.

Even in the wild, the cunning of our primate cousins, a subject of ongoing ethological and primatological study, reveals fascinating glimpses of this sophisticated strategy, demonstrating that the biological roots of strategic exploitation run deep. Chimpanzees, for instance, don't just chase monkeys haphazardly through the trees; they've been repeatedly observed engaging in highly coordinated ambush hunting, a complex social behavior that requires abstract thought, effective communication, and predictive reasoning about prey movement. Some chimpanzees act as "starters," flushing prey towards a pre-determined location or obstacle, while others position themselves as "finishers," strategically cutting off escape routes, often silently communicating through gestures or subtle vocalizations. This isn't random violence or simple pursuit; it's a planned maneuver, a living trap designed to corner, disorient, and capture prey with maximum efficiency and minimal risk to the hunters. This early form of collaborative, deceptive hunting showcases the nascent cognitive architecture for strategic thinking, demonstrating a foundational capacity to exploit the environment and the prey's predictable escape patterns, funneling resources directly into the group's grasp without requiring individual strength to overcome a nimble target. The principle here is clear: leverage intelligence and cooperation to minimize effort and maximize return, an early, amoral lesson in efficiency.

Early humans, with their rapidly developing brains and increasingly versatile, dexterous hands – capabilities that were intertwined with the evolution of bipedalism and complex tool-making, as explored in earlier chapters – perfected this primal art to an astonishing degree. They transcended the living ambush to construct physical, often concealed, mechanisms for capture. Archaeological evidence from across the globe, including vast mass kill sites in North America (such as bison jumps, where entire herds were stampeded over cliffs into natural corrals) and intricate fish weirs in coastal and riverine areas designed to funnel and hold aquatic prey, testifies to the widespread and sophisticated use of ingenious traps. They dug massive pitfalls, artfully camouflaged with branches and foliage, patiently waiting for an unsuspecting large game animal like a mammoth or bison to plunge to its doom. They crafted intricate snares from twisted plant fibers or animal sinew, and expansive nets woven with painstaking effort, understanding the behavioral patterns of their prey well enough to anticipate movement, identify choke points in the landscape, and lay a hidden, passive trap. This wasn't merely about strength or speed; it was about intelligence applied to capture. It was about foresight, understanding complex cause and effect relationships, and exploiting the environment to funnel a resource directly into one's grasp, often without direct confrontation. The development of such trapping technologies allowed for unprecedented efficiencies in hunting, providing reliable protein sources that supported larger, more sedentary populations, thus accelerating the accumulation of "bananas" beyond immediate consumption and driving further social complexity and hierarchical organization. This mastery of the physical trap was a direct extension of the amoral imperative, maximizing yield while minimizing expenditure of direct energy or risk.

Fast forward through history, through millennia of human ingenuity and escalating ambition, and this primal art of the trap metastasizes into humanity's most insidious and effective forms of "banana stealing" and resource control. We've evolved far beyond digging literal holes in the ground; now, our traps are woven from the intricate threads of psychology, law, economics, and social leverage, forming invisible yet ironclad cages around individuals and entire populations. These sophisticated traps do not rely on physical restraint but on the exploitation of deep-seated human desires, fears, cognitive biases, and systemic inequalities. The trapper always operates with an asymmetry of information or power, understanding the victim's vulnerabilities (their ignorance, desperation, greed, or yearning for belonging) better than the victim understands the nature of the trap. This evolution of the trap reflects the increasing sophistication of our amoral imperative, adapting to the complexities of human societies and their layered vulnerabilities. The trapper, driven by the ceaseless pursuit of "bananas," often rationalizes their actions through the "narrative veil," framing their exploitation as legitimate business, divine will, or natural order, thus maintaining a clear conscience even while orchestrating profound disempowerment.

Consider cult recruitment and retention strategies as a prime, chilling example of the modern psychological trap, a topic extensively studied in social psychology and sociology of religion. The "bait" is often the irresistible promise of belonging, ultimate purpose, profound answers in a chaotic world, or exclusive access to enlightenment – an alluring "banana" for the vulnerable, the searching, or the disillusioned, particularly those experiencing a crisis of identity or meaning. Recruiters, often trained in sophisticated manipulative techniques rooted in behavioral psychology, employ "love bombing" and present a false sense of instant, unconditional community, drawing individuals into a new, intensely insular social environment. Once inside, the "trap" springs with escalating demands. New identities are subtly or overtly forged through constant indoctrination and control over information, isolating the individual from external perspectives. Former connections and support networks are systematically severed (creating a profound isolation that functions as a psychological pitfall), financial resources are increasingly demanded (the slow, systematic taking of bananas, often justified as contributions to a higher cause), and dissent is stifled through pervasive indoctrination, thought-reform techniques, and the potent fear of excommunication or dire supernatural consequences. The individual is not physically restrained, but psychologically ensnared, trapped within a self-reinforcing narrative where leaving means losing everything, they've been led to believe is good, true, and essential for their very identity and salvation. The internal experience for the trapped is often one of the initial euphoria, followed by growing cognitive dissonance and a sense of helplessness as the walls of the trap close in, making escape appear impossible or catastrophic. Yet, even within these tightly controlled systems, individual cognitive dissonance can intensify, and external intervention or a critical mass of doubt can sometimes catalyze moments of profound awakening and, though immensely difficult, enable escape and recovery. The leader, the ultimate trapper and master of psychological manipulation, establishes a self-perpetuating system for perpetual "banana" transfer, consolidating power and resources under their absolute control, demonstrating the dominance imperative at its most insidious.

Similarly, colonial exploitation represents a macro-scale, historical trap, a vast, multi-generational system of "banana-stealing" that has profoundly shaped global geopolitics and wealth distribution, analyzed extensively by post-colonial studies and development economics. It begins with the initial military conquest – the physical "capture" of land and people, often justified by self-serving religious or racial superiority narratives. But the true, enduring trap lies not in the initial violence, but in the subsequent establishment of deeply entrenched, self-perpetuating systems: Economic Structures: Colonizers systematically imposed monocultures, forcing vast populations to cultivate single cash crops (like rubber, cotton, sugar, coffee) for the metropole's industries, while simultaneously demanding raw materials and actively suppressing local manufacturing. This created a profound economic trap where colonized economies became perpetual suppliers of raw "bananas," unable to consume their own produce, diversify their economies, or develop independently, remaining dependent appendices to colonial power. Indigenous industries were deliberately destroyed to eliminate competition, ensuring a captive market for goods manufactured in the colonizing nation. Legal Systems: Laws were enacted that systematically dispossessed indigenous populations of their ancestral lands, granted vast tracts of territory and resource rights exclusively to colonizers, and enforced brutal labor systems (slavery, indentured servitude, forced labor) that guaranteed cheap or free work, ensuring a continuous

flow of human "bananas." These legal frameworks were often justified by the "Narrative Veil" of civilizing missions, racial inferiority,
or the supposed "empty lands" doctrine, providing a moral veneer
for outright theft and systemic oppression, transforming the entire legal and judicial apparatus into a tool for banana acquisition
and control, a prime example of law used as a weapon. Infrastructure: Railways, ports, and roads were built not for the benefit or
development of the colonized populations, but with the precise
strategic goal of efficiently extracting resources (minerals, agricultural produce, timber) from the interior back to the metropole,
functioning as arteries of sustained "banana" drainage. The very
design of these systems ensured dependence and facilitated the
continuous flow of wealth away from the colonized. The colonized
people were not merely "stolen" from in a single, overt act; they
were caught in a vast, systemic trap designed for the continuous,
multi-generational extraction of their land, labor, and resources,
demonstrating a chilling long-term application of the amoral imperative, the echoes of which are still felt in global inequalities
today.

And in contemporary society, sophisticated financial schemes
embody perhaps the purest, most abstracted form of the "trap,"
analyzed through finance theory and behavioral economics. Ponzi
schemes, for instance, don't simply steal money; they lure victims
with the irresistible bait of impossibly high, consistent returns,
preying on greed and trust, drawing them deeper into the illusion until the entire, unsustainable structure inevitably collapses,
trapping the vast majority of late-stage investors, their "bananas"
having vanished into the pockets of the early entrants and the
architects. Predatory lending practices don't demand immediate
payment; they set a subtle trap of escalating interest rates, hidden fees, complex terms, and balloon payments that slowly but
surely strip assets from the desperate and financially vulnerable,
creating cycles of inescapable debt that function as a form of modern economic enslavement, trapping individuals and families in a

perpetual state of financial depletion. Insider trading isn't a direct grab; it's the exploitation of privileged, asymmetrical information, a strategic advantage in a complex financial landscape, allowing the privileged few to profit exponentially at the expense of unsuspecting masses who are caught in the wider, seemingly fair, but fundamentally rigged "stolen banana" game. Furthermore, even broader aspects of our globalized economy, as highlighted by critical economic theory and political economy, can be viewed as complex, multi-layered traps where wealth concentrates at the top through systemic advantages (e.g., intellectual property laws, corporate lobbying, regulatory capture, tax havens), creating a persistent funnel for "bananas" from the many to the few, without any overt act of theft, merely the clever, amoral design of the system itself, a self-perpetuating mechanism of unequal distribution. This extends even to the pervasive digital traps of our age, where algorithms and platforms are designed to exploit our attention, data, and psychological vulnerabilities for continuous behavioral and economic "banana" extraction, often turning our very engagement into a resource to be harvested.

From the ingenious pitfall dug by early hominids to the multi-layered Ponzi scheme managed by algorithms, from the strategic ambush of a chimpanzee hunting party to the systemic economic subjugation of colonial empires and the ubiquitous digital exploitation of personal data, the fundamental principle remains chillingly consistent: the amoral imperative to acquire bananas, executed not through crude, risky force, but through the sophisticated, patient, and often invisible art of the trap. It is the ultimate testament to human cunning and our unparalleled cognitive capacity, demonstrating our species' unique ability to identify, create, and relentlessly exploit the vulnerabilities of others—be they animal instincts, psychological needs, socio-economic disadvantages, informational asymmetries, or even the very architecture of modern technology—all for our own strategic gain. The trap, in its countless manifestations, reveals the pinnacle of our amoral intelligence, a quiet, calculated dominance that often goes unseen, yet shapes the very architecture of power and resource distribution in the world. Recognizing the pervasive nature of these traps, and the amoral drives that fuel their creation, is the first step towards understanding the true, often unsettling, mechanics of human behavior and societal organization. It also, crucially, informs the ongoing societal efforts to establish ethical frameworks and legal safeguards designed to mitigate their most destructive manifestations, highlighting humanity's continuous struggle to balance its inherent drives with the demands of cooperation and fairness.

Chapter Ten

The Ultimate Arena: Politics as the Grand Banana War.

We've seen it: the sentinel's gaze, perpetually locked on advan-
• tage, unerringly spots the banana. We've seen the dominance
drive, an unyielding force, compel us to seize it. This primal imperative, utterly amoral and relentless, shapes individual ambition,
carves our most ancient narratives, and forges us into fiercely
loyal, perpetually warring tribes. But if you want to understand
the raw, unvarnished truth of human collective action and conflict,
look no further than politics. From the mundane local council
meeting to the grand, glittering, often grotesque spectacles of
national capitals like Washington D.C., politics is not just a battleground for "bananas"—it is the ultimate, most sophisticated, most
brutally efficient battleground, played out on a scale that would
render our primate ancestors utterly bewildered. This arena is not
about noble ideals; it is a profound, ceaseless, and often horrifying
dance of naked power, ruthless resource acquisition, and the
inherent, utterly inescapable mechanics of human ambition. Face
it.

The journey from a chimp troop's visceral dominance hierarchy
in the jungle to the labyrinthine power struggles within any legislative body is not a metamorphosis of fundamental motivation.
It is, unequivocally, an astonishing escalation in complexity and
abstraction, a refinement of the same brutal game. The very same
primal drives that propelled an alpha chimp to the summit of

his group, granting him preferential access to mates and prime foraging grounds, are undeniably at play in the human quest for public office. The dominance drive, that innate, unyielding push for control and elevated status, manifests in politics as an insatiable, often pathological, ambition for power, fueling relentless campaigning, gladiatorial debates, and the strategic forging of ephemeral alliances that last only as long as they serve the shared grab. The visceral thrill of electoral victory represents the ultimate "top banana" in the human social and political pecking order, an addiction for those who taste its power. As illuminated by evolutionary psychology and political psychology, politicians, like their primate forebears, perpetually jockey for position, influence, and the tangible and intangible resources that flow from control (Wright; Pinker; De Waal). This relentless jockeying isn't simply about policy; it's profoundly rooted in the neurochemical rewards of elevated status – the dopamine surge from successful competition, the reduction of stress hormones like cortisol when control is achieved, and the reinforcing feedback loops that render the pursuit of power an end in itself. This is power not as a means to an end, but as a coveted "banana" in its purest, most intoxicating form, granting immediate access to an endless cascade of others. This pervasive thirst for control gives chilling credence to Robert Michels' "Iron Law of Oligarchy," which bluntly states that even purportedly democratic organizations inevitably gravitate towards rule by a select few elites, precisely because the very act of organization creates a leadership class inherently driven to perpetuate its own power and consolidate its absolute grip on the collective's "bananas." This is not a bug; it is a feature of our biological programming.

The tribalism we explored in Chapter 9, that fundamental "we vs. they" dynamic, finds its most overt, organized, and devastatingly impactful expression in modern politics. Political parties, forget what they tell you, are not merely intellectual coalitions of shared ideas or policy preferences; they are powerful, identity-defining tribes. The "we vs. they" mentality, deeply rooted in our primal group-forming instincts and magnified by cognitive biases like confirmation bias, ingroup favoritism, and outgroup derogation, becomes the dominant organizing principle of political life (Boyd and Richerson; Harari). This fosters intense, often irrational, loyalty within one's own party (the "in-group") and deep suspicion, animosity, or even outright hatred towards the opposing side (the "out-group"). As meticulously documented by sociologists studying social polarization, every policy debate, every election cycle, every public statement becomes an opportunity to fortify "our" tribe's righteousness, its moral superiority, and its exclusive claim to truth, while simultaneously demonizing "their" tribe's perceived flaws, malice, or existential threat. This dynamic is acutely, painfully evident in the increasingly polarized landscape of American politics, where party affiliation frequently dictates social circles, media consumption, and even personal values, transmogrifying political discourse into a perpetual, zero-sum banana war. The mere existence of an "out-group" fiercely galvanizes the "in-group," reinforcing cohesion and loyalty, making the political struggle not just about abstract policies, but about defending one's very identity and collective existence—a fundamental, unavoidable driver of conflict in international relations as well as domestic politics. Moreover, periods of profound crisis—be they economic downturns, social unrest, or external geopolitical threats—are not just challenges; they are opportunities that dramatically intensify this tribal polarization, providing fertile ground for political entrepreneurs to consolidate power by emphasizing an existential threat from the "other," thereby rendering the population more susceptible to amoral "banana grabs" framed as absolutely necessary measures for collective survival.

The Narrative Veil (Chapter 4), that essential human capacity to weave compelling stories that justify amoral pursuits, operates in hyperdrive within the political sphere. Ideologies—democracy, freedom, liberty, equality, patriotism, national security, social justice, individual responsibility—are constantly invoked as sacred truths, universal principles, or immutable moral imperatives. But make no mistake: under an unblinking amoral gaze, they are revealed as strategic constructs. They are grand justifications for policies transparently designed to funnel resources, power, and privilege to specific groups: wealthy donors, powerful corporations, particular demographics, or the party faithful. Communications theory and propaganda studies reveal that political messaging isn't primarily about conveying objective truth; it's about crafting emotionally resonant narratives that cunningly obscure the underlying amoral pursuits. These narratives make exploitation palatable, transform raw self-interest into perceived public service, and render the relentless pursuit of "bananas" a noble endeavor. Tax cuts for the wealthy are framed as "job creation for all," deregulation is presented as "freedom from government overreach," and social programs are demonized as "wasteful handouts" versus championed as "vital safety nets." The language of morality, patriotism, and shared values is relentlessly deployed as a powerful, persuasive tool to justify the acquisition, redistribution, and monopolization of "bananas" by one group for its own benefit, often demonstrably at the expense of another. This creates what political economists term "rent-seeking" behavior, where economic gains are secured not through productive activity but through manipulation of the political or economic environment. This masterful manipulation of narratives allows political actors to secure and expand their power and resources while appearing to serve the greater good, thereby securing public consent for their ongoing, amoral "banana grabs." The profound effectiveness of this veil is paramount: it permits political actors to execute policies driven by amoral self-interest while maintaining the societal cohesion necessary for their power to persist. This is the ultimate con.

And finally, the fine art of the trap (Chapter 10) reaches its absolute zenith in political maneuvering, where subtle, systemic mechanisms ensnare individuals and populations in a continuous cycle of resource extraction. Legislation itself is often a complex trap, intricately designed with subtle loopholes, specific exemptions, or hidden clauses that disproportionately benefit a particular industry, powerful lobbyist, or connected individual, while appearing innocuous or even broadly beneficial to the broader public. This is the essence of regulatory capture, where the very entities meant to be regulated effectively control the regulators, thereby creating a legal funnel for "bananas" at direct public expense. Within the United States, this predatory political behavior is starkly, sickeningly evident in countless instances where specific industries—notably finance, pharmaceuticals, and fossil fuels—invest colossal sums in lobbying and campaign contributions. This investment is not a charitable act; it is a cold, calculated, strategic "trap-setting" expenditure designed to secure legislative and regulatory outcomes that guarantee massive, sustained profits, often by externalizing catastrophic costs onto the public, undermining public health, or stifling genuine competition. For instance, the crafting of Medicare Part D with its specific, anti-competitive favors for drug companies, or the persistent, blatant resistance to robust climate legislation in favor of continued fossil fuel subsidies, are not accidents of policy; they are undeniable examples of policies where the public is tacitly, relentlessly forced to subsidize private gain, often without fully comprehending the systemic mechanisms at play.

Now, let's talk about the master trap, the systemic elephant in the room that often goes unaddressed in polite constitutional discourse: Administrative Law. In the United States, the very concept of separation of powers, foundational to the Constitution, is relentlessly challenged by the rise of the modern "administrative state." Agencies like the EPA, FDA, SEC, or Federal Reserve, populated by unelected bureaucrats, wield immense power that blurs the lines between legislative, executive, and even judicial functions. Congress, overwhelmed by the complexity of modern governance, has broadly delegated its law-making authority to these agencies through vague "enabling statutes." This effectively allows unelected officials to create thousands of rules and regulations that carry the force of law, bypassing the arduous, public process of congressional debate and direct accountability to the electorate. This is not some abstract legal debate; this is a direct, undeniable method by which the amoral imperative circumvents the very spirit of the Constitution. Administrative agencies not only make rules, but they also enforce them and, through Administrative Law Judges (ALJs), adjudicate disputes arising from those rules. These ALJs are not independent Article III judges; they are agency employees, inherently biased toward their own agency's position. This concentration of legislative, executive, and judicial power within a single, unelected entity is precisely what the Framers sought to prevent, yet it is now the everyday reality of governance, a massive, ongoing "banana grab" institutionalized within the system itself. This system allows for the rapid creation of rules that can funnel resources, impose burdens, or grant privileges to specific actors without the transparent, deliberative, or directly accountable processes mandated by representative democracy.

But the rot goes even deeper. It infects the very judiciary, the supposed guardians of our rights, the final arbiters of justice. The uncomfortable truth is that judges are not umpires calling balls and strikes; they are human beings with inherent biases, political leanings, and a deep-seated drive to acquire and protect their own "bananas," often at the expense of those they are sworn to serve. Studies have repeatedly shown that a judge's political affiliation significantly influences their decisions, particularly in ideologically charged cases. Judges appointed by Republican presidents often rule demonstrably differently than those appointed by Democrats, especially in cases involving abortion, affirmative action, capital punishment, and sex discrimination. This isn't about different legal interpretations; it's about the amoral imperative manifesting itself in the courtroom, where the "bananas" at stake are not just resources, but power itself: the power to shape the law, to control outcomes, and to reinforce the dominance of their own tribe. This bias seeps into every level of the judicial system. Consider the chilling scenario: a judge, before a trial even truly begins, openly states a preference for employers being able to fire employees even if they possess negotiated union rights. Then, despite a complete lack of evidence supporting the employer's case for termination, this same judge manufactures a justification—claiming the employee was "truculent," a term entirely unrelated to the facts presented—to rule in favor of the employer. This is not justice; it is a blatant, unconscionable subversion of due process and contractual rights, a raw exercise of power where a judge's pre-existing agenda directly circumvents a citizen's constitutional rights to aid in the "banana stealing" for one side. Such instances are stark evidence that the courtroom can become another arena for the amoral imperative, where politically motivated rulings on voting rights can effectively disenfranchise entire groups of citizens, or where sentencing disparities reveal ingrained biases. We are told to trust the courts, but the evidence screams otherwise: the judiciary, far from being a neutral check on power, is often another theater where the amoral imperative plays out, where the powerful protect their own, and where the constitutional rights of ordinary citizens are just another "banana" to be seized or denied.

Electoral strategies, meticulously crafted through insights from data science and computational social science, are elaborate traps designed to capture and retain power, often by brazenly disenfranchising some while consolidating the votes of others. Tactics like gerrymandering (the deliberate manipulation of electoral district boundaries to favor one party, ensuring safe seats and utterly undermining competitive elections) and voter suppression (through restrictive voter ID laws, strategic poll closures in opposition-leaning areas, aggressive purges of voter rolls, or deliberate limitations on early voting) are not accidental democratic imperfections; they are calculated, systemic traps designed to prevent specific, often marginalized, groups from accessing their political "bananas" (their vote) and thus undermine their collective power. Campaign finance laws, often presented as mechanisms to ensure fairness, can paradoxically become a trap that limits access to power for those without vast financial resources, ensuring that the "bananas" of influence flow disproportionately to the wealthy through legal, yet profoundly unequal, avenues. The pervasive "revolving door" phenomenon, where former government officials move seamlessly into high-paying lobbying jobs for the very industries they once regulated, allows individuals to directly monetize their inside knowledge and connections, creating an ongoing system of influence peddling that is inherently predatory, consistently feeding private interests at the expense of genuine public service. Politicians expertly exploit our cognitive biases, fears, and tribal loyalties, setting psychological traps that guide voters towards predetermined outcomes, ensuring the continued flow of "bananas" to those who control the levers of power. The very structure of political systems, even democracies, often contains built-in traps that serve to maintain existing power structures and make true systemic change difficult for outsiders or insurgent groups, creating a self-perpetuating cycle of elite control over the "banana supply." This is the essence of a "predator state"—a concept discussed in political economy, where the governmental apparatus becomes an explicit tool for a narrow band of elites to systematically enrich themselves through policy instruments. The constant interplay between economic power and political power forms a reinforcing loop: wealth buys influence, which in turn crafts policies that generate more wealth, creating an ever-expanding hoard of "bananas" for those at the top, a vicious cycle. This dynamic often leaves the average citizen, caught in these political traps and tribal conflicts, feeling a profound political apathy, disengagement, chronic stress from perpetual polarization, and a corrosive erosion of trust in institutions, which paradoxically can further strengthen the hand of those setting the traps, ensuring their continued reign.

From the first communal hunts for survival to the complex machinations of global governance, the underlying amoral imperative remains absolutely constant, merely adapting its methods to the ever-increasing scale and complexity of human organization. The political arena is where our evolutionary drives for dominance and resource control are most openly, most efficiently, and most ruthlessly exercised. It's where the most sophisticated traps are set, often veiled by legal jargon or benign-sounding policy, explicitly designed to extract resources; where the most convincing narrative veils are spun, transforming raw self-interest into compelling national myths; and where the ultimate, coveted banana – power over others, and thus preferential access to all other "bananas" – is fiercely, ceaselessly fought for. This struggle is waged not by moral giants, as the narrative veil would have you believe, but by exceptionally skilled, utterly amoral human apes, leveraging every psychological, sociological, economic, and technological tool at their disposal, often manipulating humanity's innate capacity for cooperation and idealism in the process. Understanding politics through this brutal, uncompromising lens, stripping away every shred of idealized rhetoric, allows us to grasp its true, relentless nature: a continuous, high-stakes battle for control over resources and the systems that allocate them, a profound demonstration of our species' unyielding drive to acquire and protect its bananas, whatever the cost, even though the systemic, often invisible, predation of its own citizens. Paradoxically, even the pursuit of these self-serving 'bananas' by the powerful can, at times, inadvertently foster collective benefits, as stable systems of extraction require a modicum of order and infrastructure that can also serve broader populations, albeit as a secondary outcome to elite consolidation. The paradox of democracy is not an anomaly; it is the ultimate testament that even within a system theoretically designed for the will of the many, the fundamental amoral drives of the few find the most elaborate and effective avenues for "banana" acquisition, continuously challenging and often overwhelming the ideals of equitable governance. This is the reality. Now you really see it unless you have self-imposed blinders on.

Chapter Eleven

The Unwritten Rule: Finders Keepers, Losers Weepers, and Its Primal Manifestation: The Five-Finger Discount.

Having ripped back the narrative veil from politics, exposing it as the ultimate banana war, we must now confront the even more pervasive, yet often unspoken, operating principle that governs so much of human interaction: "Finders Keepers, Losers Weepers." This isn't a quaint childhood rhyme; it's a ruthless, amoral ethos, an unwritten law etched into the very fabric of competitive human systems. Its understanding requires an interdisciplinary lens, drawing insights from economics, sociology, law, political science, history, and even evolutionary biology. Consider its most primal, almost instinctual form: the "five-finger discount." This isn't just a petty individual transgression; it's the raw, unadorned expression of "finders keepers" at its simplest. A coveted item is found, taken, and kept, with the "loser"—the store, the rightful owner—left to "weep" over the loss. This is the purest, most brutal articulation of the amoral imperative in action, dictating that raw success and strategic maneuvering, not ethical considerations or abstract notions of fairness, are the sole determinants of who secures and retains the "bananas"—and who is left to pick up the bitter, often devastating, consequences. This chimp-like drive for immediate resource acquisition, bypassing established rules, isn't a cultural construct unique to Western capitalism; it's a fundamental, cross-cultural constant, adapting its methodologies across millennia and continents. From ancient empires asserting dominion over conquered lands to tribal elders controlling scarce water sources, its core logic remains invariant. Prepare for it to stick directly in your face.

This core principle, "Finders Keepers, Losers Weepers," manifests relentlessly in the churning maelstrom of competitive industries. Here, it isn't merely present; it's the very algorithm driving growth, consolidation, and ruthless efficiency. Forget the polished narratives of innovation and consumer choice; the core of unbridled capitalism is a ceaseless, often zero-sum, pursuit of market share, profit maximization, and absolute dominance. This is a fundamental insight from critical economic analysis and strategic studies. Corporations, embodying the collective amoral imperative of their executives and shareholders, engage in strategic maneuvers devastatingly effective at acquiring "bananas" and annihilating competitors. Consider the stark reality of monopolies and oligopolies, where a handful of colossal entities—from tech giants like Google and Amazon, to pharmaceutical behemoths and financial conglomerates—consolidate power not merely through superior product, but by strategically acquiring or driving out any emerging rival. They "find" a burgeoning market or technology, then aggressively "keep" it by crushing nascent competition through overwhelming financial power, legal intimidation, or simply absorbing them. The smaller, often more innovative, "losers" aren't merely outcompeted; they're systemically eliminated, their efforts dissolved, their potential absorbed or suppressed, their costs externalized onto the broader economy or laid-off workers.

This extends to predatory pricing, a cold, calculated tactic where a dominant player intentionally sells products or services far below cost, not for efficiency, but to bleed smaller, often localized rivals dry until they declare bankruptcy. The "finder"—the cash-rich corporation—then reaps the monopoly rents, having eliminated all challengers, while the "loser"—the small, independent business—is wiped out. The only "ethics" at play are the often-porous legal boundaries defining "anti-competitive practices"—boundaries frequently blurred or moved by powerful lobbying. John D. Rockefeller and his predatory Standard Oil Company immediately come to mind (Marx).

Mergers and acquisitions (M&A), trumpeted as strategic growth, are frequently nothing short of sophisticated, legalized acts of corporate conquest, pure expressions of finders keepers. One company "finds" a valuable asset—be it a competitor's innovative technology, its vast customer base, or its patented processes—and "keeps" it by force of capital. The immediate consequence for the "loser"—the acquired entity—often involves mass layoffs, the dissolution of its brand, and the financial ruin of its previous owners or employees who lost their equity. These human costs are merely externalized liabilities in the ruthless pursuit of consolidated "banana" control. Moreover, the insidious reality of information asymmetry is a key weapon for the "finders." Those with superior access to market data, industry trends, or even non-public knowledge—think about the fine line with insider trading, or the early adoption advantage in emerging tech—can exploit this informational "banana" to make moves that leave less informed competitors, investors, or consumers utterly devastated, a phenomenon well-documented in financial economics and organizational theory (Friedman; The Chicago School of Economics). The complexity of modern financial instruments is itself a trap, often deliberately opaque, allowing the "finders"—sophisticated financial institutions—to extract wealth from "losers"—less informed investors or even entire economies—who can't decipher the intricate rules of the game. Even seemingly beneficial "disruptive innovation"—like Uber or Airbnb—often begins as an amoral act of circumventing existing regulations and labor laws, rapidly accumulating "bananas" by operating outside the established rules, forcing the "losers"—traditional taxi companies, hotels, unionized labor—to adapt or die. This is the unwritten rule applied to entire sectors: seize the opportunity, bypass the obstacles, and let the traditional players weep.

This ruthless ethos penetrates to the core of legal systems, often revealing justice as a far more cynical mechanism than its noble facade suggests. This is a perspective deeply explored in critical legal studies and jurisprudence (Critical Legal Studies). While constitutions and statutes are theoretically designed to ensure fairness and protect rights, the practical application of law frequently boils down to who can afford the most skilled legal predators, who possess the superior strategic acumen, and who can effectively leverage procedural "traps" to their undeniable advantage. The most glaring example is the fundamental barrier of access to justice: civil disputes, complex corporate lawsuits, and even criminal defense become battles of attrition that only the wealthy can truly afford to fight. Those who can pay for armies of lawyers and endless appeals effectively "find" favorable legal outcomes, while the less affluent "losers" are forced to settle for far less than they're due, or worse, are unjustly penalized because they can't afford a vigorous defense. This economic disparity transforms the courtroom into another marketplace for "bananas." Consider tort reform, often lobbied for by powerful corporations. While presented as a means to curb frivolous lawsuits, it frequently serves to limit the "losers'"—injured parties, victims of corporate negligence—ability to recover adequate compensation from powerful entities, essentially making it more difficult for them to "find" justice or redress. Even when legal reforms are pursued with genuine intent to level the playing field, the ingenuity of the 'finders' consistently seeks new methods to circumvent or exploit such changes, adapting the legal game to their enduring advantage.

Plea bargaining, while a necessity for an overloaded justice system, also exemplifies "finders keepers." Prosecutors, the "finders" of leverage, use the threat of harsher sentences to pressure "losers"—defendants, particularly those with limited resources or understanding—into accepting plea deals that circumvent full trials and often result in convictions or disproportionate penalties, even for the innocent. Beyond the courtroom, legal "traps" designed by the powerful are endemic. Regulatory loopholes and the strategic use of offshore tax havens are prime examples: wealthy individuals and corporations pay legions of lawyers and accountants to "find" legal avenues to avoid contributing their share to the public good, leaving the burden disproportionately on "losers"—average taxpayers, underfunded public services—to pay for societal infrastructure. The "finders" keep their enormous wealth, the "losers" bear the cost. Furthermore, legal fictions like corporate personhood and the pervasive influence of regulatory capture and lobbying on legislative processes grant corporations immense power to shape laws and regulations specifically to their "finders keepers" advantage, ensuring that the rules of the game are written by those who benefit most from its ruthless application. The legal system, far from being a neutral arbiter, frequently serves as a highly effective mechanism for reallocating "bananas" to those best equipped to play the brutal game, reinforcing pre-existing power imbalances—a conclusion borne out by sociological studies of stratification and power structures (Weber; Bourdieu; Social Dominance Theory).

Beyond boardrooms and courtrooms, "Finders Keepers, Losers Weepers" permeates broader social interactions, shaping everything from mundane daily encounters to the entrenched architecture of systemic inequalities. Observe how opportunities often accrue disproportionately to those who are simply "present" at the right time, who possess existing social capital and extensive networks, or who are willing to push ethical boundaries others deem unacceptable. Consider the historical and ongoing reality of land grabs, whether driven by colonial expansion, the devastating effects of manifest destiny, or the modern, insidious march of gentrification—phenomena analyzed through historical, anthropological, and urban studies (Diamond; Rodney; Wallerstein). Those who find the land, the resources, or the opportunity, through force, legal maneuvering, or sheer economic leverage, relentlessly keep it. The original inhabitants, or less powerful claimants, are left to weep, displaced and dispossessed. This ruthless pattern is replicated in countless social micro-interactions: who gets the promotion in a competitive workplace, who secures the coveted public resource in a time of scarcity, who even receives preferential treatment in a crowded marketplace or administrative queue. It's rarely about who is most deserving by some objective moral standard. Instead, it's about who is most assertive, who has the best connections, who understands the unspoken, often amoral, rules of the game, or who is simply willing to take the biggest risks—and absorb the potential fallout. The amoral imperative doesn't care for fairness; it rewards the effective, often ruthless, acquisition of "bananas." This extends directly to the perpetuation of social stratification: once "bananas"—wealth, status, opportunity, inherited privilege—are accumulated by one group or family, powerful mechanisms, both overt and subtle, are deployed to "keep" them, ensuring that those who started with less are systemically prevented from "finding" similar opportunities, creating an enduring, often self-reinforcing, cycle of privilege for the "finders" and perpetual disadvantage for the "weepers" (Weber; Bourdieu; Social Dominance Theory). This can manifest as rigid caste systems, inherited noble titles, or simply the perpetuation of dynastic wealth and influence, deeply embedded across diverse societies and historical periods. Critical "bananas" like quality education, comprehensive healthcare, and even basic personal security become commodities disproportionately "kept" by those who already possess them, intensifying the "losers weepers" dynamic across generations and solidifying entrenched power. Despite periodic societal convulsions or movements seeking redistribution, the core mechanisms of 'finders keepers' often prove remarkably resilient, re-establishing themselves in new guises to perpetuate the advantage of the privileged. Even the digital divide and control over information represent a modern iteration: those who "find" access to technology and wield the power of information manipulate narratives and control discourse, leaving those without such access as "losers" in the global information economy (Foucault; Chomsky). And in times of crisis—natural disasters, pandemics, wars—the "Finders Keepers" ethos is brutally amplified. Opportunists "find" ways to profit from public desperation through price gouging, speculation, or even vaccine hoarding, while the "losers"—the suffering populace—bear the brunt of the hardship and loss, often paying inflated prices for basic necessities, or worse, losing their lives due to engineered scarcity (Klein).

Now, let's shatter any lingering illusion that this is merely a peculiar byproduct of Western economic or political philosophy. The "Finders Keepers, Losers Weepers" ethos is a universal, cross-cultural constant, not merely present but fundamental to the competitive dynamics found in all human societies, simply adapting its tools and narrative veils to the specific historical and societal context. This conclusion emerges from a multidisciplinary examination of human history and social organization. From the earliest tribal societies where control over prime hunting grounds or water sources was violently asserted and maintained by the strongest, to the elaborate hierarchies of feudalism, this principle reigned supreme. In feudal Europe, the lord or king "found"—often by conquest or decree—vast tracts of land and populations of serfs, and they "kept" them through a brutal system of fealty and force. The "losers"—the peasants—were bound to the land, their labor exploited, their freedoms non-existent. This wasn't a moral compact; it was a pure "banana" arrangement. Colonialism and imperialism provide perhaps the most grotesque global manifestation. European powers, driven by the amoral imperative for resources and expansion, "found" vast continents teeming with wealth and indigenous populations. They then "kept" these territories and their riches through brute military force, sophisticated legal fictions, and the systematic decimation of local cultures, leaving entire civilizations as "weepers," their resources plundered, their societies fractured, their dignity stripped. This was global-scale "finders keepers."

In modern authoritarian regimes and kleptocracies, the principle is even more nakedly applied. Elites "find" control of state apparatuses—ministries, state-owned enterprises, natural resources—and then proceed to "keep" these national "bananas" through corruption, nepotism, and ruthless suppression of dissent (Mosca; Pareto; Machiavelli). The populace are the ultimate "losers," stripped of their wealth, their rights, and often their very voice. Even in seemingly rule-bound international relations, the "Finders Keepers, Losers Weepers" dynamic plays out in geopolitical competition. Nations "find" strategic alliances, control over vital choke points—like maritime trade routes—or access to critical resources—oil, rare earth minerals—and then fiercely "keep" these advantages, often at the expense of weaker nations. The phenomenon of debt traps, where powerful nations or international financial institutions lend money to developing countries under terms that render them perpetually indebted, is a sophisticated form of "finders keepers," transforming economic assistance into a mechanism for acquiring long-term control and influence, leaving debtor nations as perpetual "weepers" struggling for true sovereignty. In every instance, regardless of the cultural or political framework, the underlying amoral imperative of 'finders keepers' remains the engine driving the allocation and consolidation of power and resources.

Ultimately, the argument becomes undeniable: in the vast, relentless expanse of human competitive endeavor, as illuminated by converging insights from economics, law, sociology, history, and political science, raw success and strategic maneuvering are the only true determinants of who keeps the "bananas" and who suffers the consequences. Ethics, morality, and justice aren't guiding principles; they're invoked as narrative veils, as high-minded justifications, or as rhetorical weapons in the ongoing struggle. But when the dust settles, when the deals are done, and when the verdicts are rendered, it's the one who masterfully navigated the traps, exploited the loopholes, outmaneuvered the opposition, or simply had the greater underlying power—the true "finder"—who walks away with the prize. The "loser" isn't compensated for their moral righteousness; they're simply left to endure the brutal reality of having been outmaneuvered, outspent, or out-strategized. This unwritten rule, "Finders Keepers, Losers Weepers," is the stark, brutal, and utterly amoral truth of our world, a direct, unfiltered manifestation of the amoral imperative's unyielding reign. This is how the system actually works.

Chapter Twelve

The "What's In It For Me?" Machine: The Engine of Human Progress (and Destruction)

We have dismantled the grand political theater, revealing its banana wars, and laid bare the brutal "Finders Keepers, Losers Weepers" ethos that dictates reality in competitive realms. Now, we must confront the most fundamental, most insidious truth about human motivation itself: the "What's In It For Me?" (WIIFM) machine. This isn't a theory; it is the silent, relentless engine that drives virtually every action, every decision, every monumental stride forward and every catastrophic descent into exploitation and conflict. Forget the comforting fictions of pure altruism, collective good, or moral imperative as primary drivers. These are, overwhelmingly, mere narrative veils. At its core, every individual, every corporation, every nation-state, every social movement, and even every familial unit is propelled by a calculation, conscious or unconscious, of self-interest—a relentless pursuit of their own "bananas." This pursuit is inherently transactional: everything gets bartered, and everything has a transactional value. From the grandest geopolitical alliances to the most intimate personal relationships, something is always being exchanged, always being valued, always being sought. This is the engine of our species, simultaneously capable of breathtaking progress and unspeakable destruction. This is not culturally relative; it is a universal, evolutionary constant. Face this raw truth.

This core transactional dynamic, the WIIFM machine, is undeniably the driving force behind much of what we laud as human progress, particularly in innovation and economic growth. The inventor isn't primarily driven by a burning desire to benefit humanity; they are driven by the prospect of fame, fortune, recognition, or the sheer intellectual "banana" of solving a complex problem. From the earliest hominid who chipped a sharper stone tool to secure more game (more "bananas" – a direct transaction of effort for sustenance), to the engineers of the Industrial Revolution who bartered new technologies for wealth and power, to modern tech moguls building empires, the underlying motive is gain. Patents and intellectual property laws exist precisely because they offer an exclusive "banana" to the "finder" of a new idea, creating a powerful economic incentive—a personalized "WIIFM" payoff—that spurs continuous, costly, and often failure-ridden development. Without the potential for individual or collective reward (even in open-source communities, contributors often "barter" their skills and time for reputation, skill development, or future job prospects – their own unique "bananas" of social capital and career advancement), the relentless grind of innovation would grind to a halt. Consider even the global space race of the Cold War; while framed as scientific advancement, it was fundamentally a WIIFM calculation for national prestige, technological superiority, and geopolitical advantage – these intangible "bananas" were bartered for immense public investment and human risk. Economic growth, the bedrock of modern prosperity across diverse economic systems, is fundamentally powered by individual and corporate self-interest. Adam Smith's "invisible hand," often sanitized into a benign force, is actually a colossal WIIFM machine built on continuous transactions. The baker doesn't bake bread out of benevolence for the community; he bakes it to make money. The entrepreneur doesn't build a business out of abstract goodwill; they build it to accumulate wealth, power, and influence. The competition between businesses to capture market share, to offer more compelling products, or to reduce costs, while resulting in benefits for consumers (a byproduct, not the primary intent), is driven by the stark reality that success means more "bananas" for the "finders" and failure means "weeping." This relentless pursuit of profit and accumulation of capital, through countless bartered transactions, has demonstrably lifted billions out of poverty and spawned technological marvels like global communication net-works and medical breakthroughs. But make no mistake, these are not altruistic triumphs; they are the emergent properties of billions of individual WIIFM calculations, a testament to the amoral imperative's efficiency in resource allocation, however unevenly distributed. Even in seemingly collectivist societies, the WIIFM op-erates at the group level—what's in it for our family, our tribe, our nation—still a form of self-interest, just aggregated, and still manifested through complex transactional relationships where loyalty, effort, or conformity are bartered for security, identity, or collective advancement.

Yet, the very same WIIFM machine that fuels progress is also the engine of widespread exploitation and conflict, leading to devastating consequences on a planetary scale. The drive to maxi-mize one's own "bananas" inevitably clashes with the similar drive of others, leading to zero-sum games where one's gain neces-sitates another's loss. This is where the transactional value of non-material assets becomes brutally clear. Exploitation of la-bor, rampant throughout history from ancient slavery to modern sweatshops, is a quintessential example: owners and corpora-tions, driven by profit (WIIFM for themselves, their shareholders, and executives), ruthlessly minimize labor costs, often leading to suppressed wages, dangerous working conditions, and the outsourcing of jobs to regions with minimal worker protections. The "banana" of increased profit for the company is bartered for the laborer's lost dignity, safety, and economic security. Environmental destruction operates on the same principle: industries pollute waterways, clear forests, strip-mine landscapes, and emit greenhouse gases not out of malice, but because externalizing these costs (i.e., making society or the planet "weep" for their "banana") is more profitable than investing in sustainable practices. This is the Tragedy of the Commons writ large, where individual WIIFM inevitably depletes a shared resource because the transactional value of immediate gain outweighs the collective, diffuse cost. The short-term "banana" of reduced operational expense is bartered for the long-term, distributed cost of ecological collapse. This logic extends globally, fueling resource conflicts where nations, driven by their geopolitical and economic WIIFM, wage proxy wars or direct interventions to secure control over oil, minerals, water, or strategic trade routes. These are rarely purely ideological clashes; they are fundamentally battles over who gets to "find" and "keep" the most valuable global "bananas" by bartering peace for dominance, or human lives for territorial control, leaving entire regions devastated, their populations as collateral "losers." The unchecked pursuit of self-interest, often enabled by technological advancement, leads to systemic inequalities and destructive competition, precisely because everything has a price, and some are willing to pay it with others' suffering. Consider financial crises like the 2008 meltdown, driven by the WIIFM calculations of bankers seeking massive bonuses, traders pursuing high-risk profits, and ratings agencies seeking fees. Their immediate "bananas" were bartered for a systemic collapse, externalizing the colossal "weeping" onto taxpayers and homeowners.

Nowhere is the WIIFM machine's insidious duality and the transactional nature of all value more starkly revealed than in the chilling dynamics of cults, a phenomenon observable across diverse cultures and historical periods. These tightly controlled social structures offer a microcosm of the amoral imperative at its most concentrated and manipulative. From the outside, the devotion of cult members appears irrational, often self-destructive, driven by an almost supernatural delusion. But under the unblinking lens of WIIFM, a cold, calculated logic emerges for every participant. For the cult leader, the motivation is almost invariably a potent cocktail of power, absolute control, immense wealth, and often sexual gratification. These are their ultimate "bananas," acquired through a direct, albeit often unspoken, transaction. The allure of absolute authority, of having disciples who cater to every whim, provides immense psychological and material rewards for individuals often marked by narcissism, grandiosity, and a profound desire for validation. The financial "bananas" can be enormous, extracted through tithes, property seizures, forced labor of followers, or even sex trafficking. The charismatic leader, a master manipulator of the narrative veil, explicitly frames the cult as the sole dispenser of vital "bananas." Consider figures like Jim Jones, who bartered a sense of belonging for ultimate control, leading to the Jonestown massacre; Shoko Asahara of Aum Shinrikyo, who offered spiritual power in exchange for absolute obedience and resources for world domination; or leaders of NXIVM, who amassed wealth and sexual control by bartering false promises of empowerment for their victims' loyalty and bodies. Their entire operation is predicated on a ruthless WIIFM calculation: how can I maximize my personal gain (power, wealth, absolute control) by exploiting and manipulating the inherent human desires of others, seeing every aspect of their followers' lives as having transactional value?

Conversely, the cult members are just as thoroughly driven by their own profound WIIFM calculations, however desperately unfulfilled their lives may have been before recruitment. For them, the "bananas" being sought are often intangible but intensely powerful: a desperate search for belonging in a world of alienation, a yearning for purpose in an existence perceived as meaningless, the promise of certainty and simple answers in an era of overwhelming complexity and doubt, or a perceived shortcut to salvation, enlightenment, or even worldly success and power (if they can align with the "chosen" few) that they cannot find elsewhere. Many seek an escape from personal trauma, grief, loneliness, or societal pressures, viewing the cult as a benevolent protector or a unique path to their ultimate "banana." The leader, employing techniques like "love bombing" and "thought reform," initially provides a strong hit of these desired "bananas"—unconditional acceptance, clear directives, a sense of specialness—creating a powerful psychological hook. In this transaction, members "barter" their time, labor, money, relationships, and eventually their autonomy and critical thinking for these perceived benefits. This creates a deeply symbiotic, yet ultimately parasitic, relationship. The leader's self-interest (power, wealth) feeds off the members' self-interest (belonging, purpose, certainty), trapping both in a system where the leader gains tangible "bananas" and the members often receive only fleeting, manufactured illusions. Behavioral psychology reveals how cognitive biases like confirmation bias (selectively seeking information that affirms cult beliefs), sunk cost fallacy (investing more to justify past sacrifices), and desire for cognitive closure (a need for definitive answers) entrench members further, continually re-evaluating the transactional value of their sacrifices against the promised "bananas." The "losers" are inevitably the members, stripped of their autonomy, their material possessions, and sometimes their lives, all while pursuing a "banana" that was never truly there for them.

This WIIFM machine, where everything gets bartered and has a transactional value, is therefore the true engine of human enterprise, churning out both breathtaking innovation and devastating exploitation with cold, amoral efficiency. It is the fundamental drive that allows for the creation of new technologies, the expansion of economies, and the organization of complex societies. Yet, it is the exact same drive that leads to ruthless competition, systemic inequality, and the subjugation of the many by the few. There is no inherent "good" or "evil" in its operation; there is only the relentless pursuit of self-interest, the ceaseless drive to acquire and protect one's own "bananas" by any effective means, always through some form of exchange. Whether in the individualistic pursuit of wealth in capitalist societies where labor is bartered for wages, the familial unit's drive for honor and resources in collectivist cultures where social support is bartered for conformity, or the tribal quest for dominance over hunting grounds where strength is bartered for survival, WIIFM is the underlying, invariant force. Game theory models demonstrate how rational self-interest, pursued individually through a series of exchanges, can lead to Nash equilibria that are collectively suboptimal but perfectly logical for each participant seeking their own "banana." Understanding this ubiquitous principle—that every decision, from the boardroom to the bedroom, from ancient tribal conflict to modern global competition, is fundamentally rooted in "what's in it for me" and involves a calculation of transactional value—is not cynicism; it is the essential prerequisite to grasping the true, amoral nature of our species and the world we have constructed. It challenges the very notion of pure altruism as a primary driver, revealing it often as a secondary outcome or a sophisticated form of indirect self-interest (e.g., social recognition, reduced cognitive dissonance), a subtle barter for internal "bananas." Now you understand the engine, stripped bare, its transactional heart laid open.

Chapter Thirteen

The Bonobo Paradox: Is Cooperation Just Another Path to More Bananas?

We've systematically dismantled the edifice of morality, revealing the amoral imperative driving human action from individual acquisition to global economic and political traps. We've unmasked the "What's In It For Me?" (WIIFM) machine as the true engine of progress and destruction, and we've recognized that everything, fundamentally, carries a transactional value—a value often shaped by the cultural frameworks that define what a "banana" truly is. Yet, a persistent counter-argument remains, often championed by proponents of inherent human goodness: the bonobo. Often presented as the "empathic ape" or the "make-love-not-war" primate, bonobos stand in stark contrast to their more aggressive chimpanzee cousins. They are known for their peaceful, matriarchal societies, their extensive use of sexual behavior to diffuse tension and form bonds, and their seemingly innate capacity for empathy, sharing, and cooperation.

Doesn't the existence of the bonobo, with its seemingly altruistic nature, fundamentally challenge the notion of humanity as a species primarily driven by amoral self-interest and banana acquisition? Doesn't it suggest a deeper, kinder current beneath our aggressive veneer? Through the unblinking lens of our amoral reckoning, the answer is both yes and, more importantly, no. To truly understand this, we must first recognize a fundamental divergence rooted not in inherent moral disposition, but in brute environmental necessity, among other contributing evolutionary and social factors. Chimpanzees, our closest relatives, typically inhabit environments where food resources are more scattered, seasonal, and unpredictable, often requiring aggressive competition, male-dominated coalitions, and even lethal inter-group violence to secure scarce "bananas." Their aggression is a rational, though brutal, strategy for survival in a challenging, highly competitive landscape. Bonobos, however, evolved in a more stable and abundant ecological niche, primarily in the Congo basin south of the Congo River, where lush, year-round fruiting vegetation and fewer large predators meant a consistently high availability of food. This stark difference in their environmental challenge is a key factor. Bonobos didn't choose peace out of inherent goodness; their environment allowed and rewarded cooperation. Their peace isn't an absence of the banana imperative, but a more efficient method of securing it collectively, minimizing costly internal strife to maximize group-level success in an environment that provided the conditions for such a strategy to flourish. It's an investment, a sophisticated transaction of immediate gratification or potential conflict for long-term, more secure, collective "bananas." What appears as genuine altruism is, in fact, a highly evolved form of self-interest, whether for individual survival, genetic propagation, or the psychological rewards of social connection, optimized for their specific ecological reality.

Consider their pervasive use of sexual behavior to resolve conflicts and reinforce social bonds. While it appears purely hedonistic, this complex social lubricant is a profoundly pragmatic evolutionary tool, a transactional currency of social cohesion. In an environment where food is plentiful, the primary threat shifts from external resource scarcity to internal group cohesion. By diffusing tension and solidifying alliances through sexual interactions, bonobos prevent destructive internal "banana wars" within the group, minimizing costly physical confrontations that drain energy, inflict injury, and divert resources. This is a far more efficient path to securing shared "bananas" than the aggressive dominance displays and violent conflicts common among chimpanzees struggling over limited resources. An internally cohesive, peaceful troop is far more effective at foraging for food, defending territory from rival groups, avoiding predators, and successfully raising offspring. The harmony within directly enables strength without. It's a calculated investment in collective banana security, minimizing costly internal strife to maximize group-level success. This parallels human behaviors where shared pleasurable experiences, from communal feasts and religious rituals to recreational activities and even forms of substance use, serve as potent social bonding agents, creating trust and solidarity that can be leveraged for collective gain—more bananas down the line. It's a fundamental recognition that the immediate cost of internal conflict vastly outweighs the longer-term cost of shared pleasure, making the latter a shrewd amoral investment. The very act of bonding, from a neurobiological perspective, releases oxytocin and dopamine, providing an internal "banana" of pleasure and well-being that reinforces cooperative behavior, making it intrinsically desirable. This neurological reward system isn't a sign of moral purity; it's the biological mechanism that efficiently facilitates the transactional value of social cohesion, a strategy perfectly suited to their abundant environment.

Similarly, the celebrated empathy and sharing among bonobos serve a distinct strategic purpose, embodying the principle of reciprocal altruism. In an environment where food is readily available, the focus shifts from fierce individual acquisition to efficient group distribution and maintenance. When a bonobo shares food with a less fortunate member or comforts a distressed companion, these actions aren't selfless deviations from WIIFM; they foster deep social connections and create an implicit, powerful system of debt and credit within the troop. From an amoral perspective, this is a calculated investment: individuals gain by helping others, with the unspoken expectation of receiving support, comfort, or resources in return when their own needs arise. Such behaviors build reputation within the social hierarchy, increase one's social capital (a valuable non-material "banana" that can be bartered for future favors or protection), and strengthen the overall group's resilience against external threats. A united, cooperative group, where individuals willingly contribute to the common good, is demonstrably better equipped to collectively acquire resources and defend them against external competition. This ultimately leads to a larger, more stable supply of bananas for all members of the in-group. This isn't kindness for kindness' sake; it's a highly efficient form of risk management and resource optimization, where a small "sacrifice" today is transacted for greater collective and individual security tomorrow. The cost of non-cooperation within such a system is severe, leading to social ostracism, reduced access to shared resources, and increased vulnerability to external threats—a direct denial of crucial "bananas," effectively enforcing cooperation through calculated self-interest.

The "hidden cost" of the Bonobo Paradox, from an amoral standpoint, is that their empathy and cooperation are overwhelmingly directed inward, towards their immediate social group. While peaceful and cooperative among themselves, bonobos are not entirely devoid of internal conflict, and their interactions with other bonobo groups, while less violent than chimpanzees, still involve avoidance or subtle competition. They are fundamentally driven by the need to secure their group's resources, often at the subtle or direct expense of other bonobo groups or rival species. Their internal peace, fostered by environmental abundance, is a powerful force that maximizes their group's ability to thrive in a competitive ecosystem by making them a more formidable, resource-acquiring unit. They cooperate to compete more effectively. This fierce in-group cohesion, a universal human trait observed across cultures from tribal formations to modern nationalisms, often translates to suspicion, competition, or even aggression towards out-groups. Cooperation within the tribe directly enhances its ability to wage banana wars against other tribes. The principle of "survival of the fittest" in an evolutionary context has never solely meant brute strength; it has increasingly emphasized adaptability, social intelligence, and, crucially, the capacity for sophisticated cooperation as a paramount form of fitness. Groups that master cooperation out-compete those that don't, ensuring their genes, and thus their strategies, propagate, reflecting the optimal amoral path for their given environmental context.

Humans exhibit this nuanced form of "cooperation for bananas" on an unparalleled scale, a testament to the amoral imperative's extraordinary adaptability. Our most complex societies, our most intricate scientific endeavors, our most widespread acts of charity, our most enduring institutions—all rely on intricate webs of cooperation and empathy. But these traits are rarely, if ever, deployed in a vacuum of self-interest. We form businesses to collectively acquire wealth, sharing tasks and expertise because the collective "banana" is larger than any individual could acquire alone. This is evident in the vast, interconnected global supply chains and complex financial markets, where millions cooperate across continents, each segment driven by its precise WIIFM calculation, performing its transactional part for the overall flow of "bananas." Crucially, while this cooperation maximizes collective output, the distribution of these "bananas" often reflects underlying power dynamics and systemic inequalities. We build political alliances and engage in democratic processes not out of pure civic virtue, but because cooperation with like-minded groups can secure power and resources that benefit our own faction or interest group; legislative bargaining is a direct, transactional exchange of votes and concessions for policy "bananas." International treaties, ostensibly for global good, are complex agreements where nations barter sovereignty or resources for security, trade advantages, or influence—pure transactional cooperation for national "bananas." We create social safety nets and welfare states that appear altruistic, but they ultimately protect our own kind (the in-group) and ensure societal stability, which in turn secures our individual resources and reduces social unrest that could threaten our existing "banana" supply. Even our seemingly most altruistic acts, such as charity or philanthropy, often come with implicit WIIFM benefits: tax benefits, enhanced social status and reputation, the profound psychological reward of feeling "good" (an internal dopamine "banana"), or the cultivation of a positive public image for corporations that can translate into consumer loyalty and increased profits. Historically, from communal hunting societies that cooperated for survival and shared resources (transaction: individual effort for collective bounty), to elaborate gift economies (transaction: generosity for status and social obligation) like the Native American Potlatch or the Kula Ring of the Trobriand Islanders, human cooperation has always been about mutually beneficial exchange, even if the "currency" was social rather than monetary. In these systems, giving away perceived wealth was a means of acquiring immense social power, reputation, and the assurance of future reciprocity—all valuable "bananas." The very formation of formal institutions and laws can be seen as an amoral mechanism to reduce the transactional costs and risks of cooperation, establishing clear rules for the exchange of "bananas" and consequences for defection, making sustained cooperation more efficient.

Game Theory provides a powerful lens through which to understand this. Concepts like the Iterated Prisoner's Dilemma demonstrate that while defection might offer a short-term gain, sustained cooperation ("Tit-for-Tat" strategies, for instance) leads to a far greater, more reliable, and mutually beneficial accumulation of "bananas" over time. Cooperation isn't moral; it's often the most rational strategy for long-term self-interest. Elinor Ostrom's seminal work on governing common pool resources showed that com-

munities successfully manage shared resources not by abandoning self-interest, but by creating rules and institutions that align
individual WIIFM with the collective good, making it personally
beneficial to cooperate and detrimental to defect. Even the neurological basis of empathy, involving mirror neurons and shared
emotional responses, serves a pragmatic purpose: understanding
another's state allows for more effective prediction of behavior,
more accurate negotiation, and more efficient manipulation or
cooperation—all geared towards optimal "banana" acquisition.

But what about the seemingly selfless acts of parental sacrifice
or the ultimate self-abnegation of heroes and martyrs? Even these
can be viewed through the amoral lens. Parental love, while profound, is deeply rooted in the evolutionary imperative for gene
propagation—a powerful "WIIFM" for one's genetic legacy. The immense psychological "bananas" derived from nurturing offspring,
combined with the biological drive to ensure the survival of one's
lineage, make such sacrifices not only rational but profoundly
rewarding from an amoral perspective. The parent's well-being
is intrinsically linked to the offspring's survival; their efforts are
an investment in their own biological continuity. Similarly, heroes and martyrs, while celebrated for their apparent selflessness, are often driven by powerful internal "bananas": an unwavering commitment to a cause or group that provides ultimate
meaning, a desire for honor, legacy, or an internal identity that
makes life unlivable if certain principles are violated. For them, the
internal "banana" of integrity, moral consistency (as they define
it), or the hope of a greater reward (be it spiritual or historical
recognition) outweighs the transactional value of their physical
life in that moment. Their choice is still a form of WIIFM, albeit
one that values abstract, internal "bananas" above all else, often
making a final, profound transaction of self for concept. This also
highlights how social norms and rituals are carefully constructed
to enforce cooperation, making non-cooperation costly through
shaming, ostracism, or reputational damage, thereby denying fu-

ture "bananas." These are subtle social contracts, transactions of conformity for acceptance and access.

Thus, the Bonobo Paradox doesn't contradict the amoral imperative; it exemplifies its adaptive genius. Cooperation and empathy aren't purely moral virtues, but rather highly refined, evolutionarily successful strategies that enable a group, and by extension its individuals, to more efficiently navigate competition, avoid costly internal conflict, and ultimately, secure a larger, more stable supply of bananas in a complex world. They are the ultimate testament to the transactional nature of all human interaction, where even our deepest bonds and seemingly selfless acts can be viewed as sophisticated exchanges, aimed at maximizing our individual and collective "bananas." We cooperate because, for complex social animals in a competitive environment, it's simply the most effective way to win the banana war. The Bonobo Paradox doesn't reveal inherent human goodness; it reveals inherent human shrewdness—the amoral imperative at its most cunning, collaborative, and pervasive. This perspective is not intended as a moral judgment or a prescription for behavior, but rather as a descriptive framework for understanding the underlying motivations that shape our actions and societies.

Chapter Fourteen

Echoes of Ape-ocalypse: Our Inevitable Future in an Amoral World.

W e have journeyed through the primal drives of the sentinel's gaze and the dominance imperative, examined the tools we wield, and dissected the intricate traps we set for bananas, from familial conflict to global economic hoarding. We even confronted the seemingly benign nature of cooperation, revealing its own strategic, amoral underpinnings. We understand now that bonobos, in their environmental niche, merely found a different, more efficient path to collective "bananas," not a moral transcendence. Now, as we stand before the mirror, stripped of our comforting moral illusions, a chilling question arises, one that an informed mind cannot avoid: If morality is truly a human invention, a mere narrative veil to justify our primal urges, are we, the naked apes, doomed to repeat endless cycles of violence, resource depletion, and self-destruction, culminating in our own Ape-ocalypse? This isn't a theological question; it's a cold, statistical projection based on the amoral calculus of our species.

The stark image of a Planet of the Apes—a world scarred by the self-inflicted wounds of a technologically advanced, yet fundamentally amoral, species—ceases to be mere science fiction. It becomes a chillingly logical, arguably inevitable, projection of our current trajectory. The desolate beaches, the ruins of a once-proud civilization, the reversion to primal, tribalistic struggles for survival – this is not a fantasy, but the predictable end-state when a species, driven by the relentless "What's In It For Me?" (WIIFM) machine (Chapter 13), sheds its fragile narrative veils (Chapter 2) or, more insidiously, uses them to rationalize its destructive impulses (Chapter 4), operating purely on the amoral imperative. If the "great illusion" of morality offers no true check on our relentless "banana stealing" (Chapter 1), but merely provides a convenient justification for it, what genuine brakes remain? The terrifying answer, from an amoral perspective, is none that we have consistently or reliably deployed. The "ape-ocalypse" is not a judgment; it is a calculation, the ultimate outcome of millions of individual WIIFM equations operating without an overarching, biologically enforced, species-level imperative.

The unvarnished conclusion of unchecked "banana stealing" on a global scale is not a moral catastrophe; it is a predictable, inexorable outcome. Our species, equipped with an unparalleled toolkit (Chapter 7) and amplified by sophisticated systems, has become astonishingly efficient at extracting resources. We've mastered the art of the trap (Chapter 10) to such a degree that we're no longer just trapping game; we're trapping entire ecosystems, extracting minerals, clear-cutting forests, and draining oceans with insatiable efficiency. The consequences—accelerating climate disruption, mass extinction, irreversible environmental degradation, and the breaching of crucial planetary boundaries—are not a failure of ethics, but the logical byproducts of an amoral imperative for limitless acquisition colliding with finite planetary resources. This is the "Finders Keepers, Losers Weepers" (Chapter 13) rule being applied to Earth itself, with future generations, other species, and the very stability of our biosphere cast as the ultimate "weepers." The haunting image of the ruined Statue of Liberty, half-buried in sand, is the ultimate testament to a civilization that, like an insatiably greedy ape troop, stripped its own planetary tree bare, leaving behind only the desiccated remnants of its former glory, a monument to its own amoral efficiency. We are rapidly creating the environmental preconditions for a world where humanity, or its evolved descendants, might indeed be reduced to warring factions scavenging among ruins, much like the disparate ape tribes. This isn't an abstract future; it's the Great Acceleration of human impact culminating in a self-made ecological trap, a direct consequence of a globalized Tragedy of the Commons where every actor prioritizes immediate WIIFM over shared long-term viability.

Furthermore, the ultimate hoard (Chapter 12) continues to consolidate, not just materially but in terms of data, influence, and predictive power. The political and economic systems we've built, rather than curbing the dominance drive, often supercharge it, rewarding extreme accumulation and brutal competition. This leads to ever-widening inequality, creating vast disparities in "banana access" both within and between human tribes (Chapter 9). This is the exact societal stratification that fuels the ape-ocalypse: a powerful few (the technologically advanced chimps/gorillas in power, or the human elites with their exclusive access to resources and information) hoarding resources and knowledge, while the rest (the primitive humans in their cages, or the subservient ape castes, representing the global disenfranchised) are left to languish, denied their essential "bananas." As the pressure on dwindling resources increases—think impending water wars, conflicts over arable land, or the scramble for rare earth minerals—and as the narrative veils justifying this inequality begin to fray, the likelihood of more intense banana wars—from internal civil unrest to geopolitical conflicts over territory, water, or energy—becomes not a possibility, but a certainty. These are the conflicts that precede, and ultimately define, the ape-ocalypse: the fragmented, desperate struggles over diminishing returns, where trust breaks down, and every interaction becomes a zero-sum game for the last crumbs of "banana." Without a genuine, internal, biologically enforced brake on our acquisitive and dominating drives, there is nothing to prevent us from cannibalizing our own species in the pursuit of the last, most prized bananas.

The echoes of the "ape-ocalypse" are already resounding, not as a distant future, but as an accelerating present, a continuous series of "mini-ape-ocalypses" throughout human history. We see them in the collapse of ancient civilizations like Easter Island, the Roman Empire, or the Maya, which succumbed to a combination of internal strife, environmental degradation, and resource mismanagement—all driven by the same fundamental WIIFM calculations that prioritize short-term gain over long-term stability. We see them today in the escalating tribalism (Chapter 9) that renders nations ungovernable, where factions, much like warring gorilla and chimpanzee troops, prioritize in-group WIIFM above any collective human good, leading to political gridlock and societal fragmentation. We observe it in the relentless pursuit of profit at the expense of planetary health, where corporations and consumers alike engage in the ultimate "banana stealing," rationalized by economic growth narratives (Chapter 4). We witness it in the technological innovations that simultaneously promise progress and forge new, more efficient weapons of self-destruction. The very tools (Chapter 7) that define our advancement – nuclear weapons, advanced bio-engineering, autonomous AI systems – are not inherently good or evil; they are amoral extensions of our WIIFM, capable of exponentially amplifying our capacity for "banana acquisition" or, tragically, for self-inflicted annihilation. The original Planet of the Apes film series explicitly linked human self-destruction to nuclear war, a direct consequence of unchecked geopolitical banana wars. Today, the specter of genetically engineered pandemics, the use of information warfare and propaganda to manipulate public perception and accelerate fragmentation, and the rise of surveillance capitalism which traps human attention and data for profit, all represent new, equally terrifying pathways to that same desolate future. Even advanced genetic engineering (like CRISPR), while promising cures, also presents the terrifying potential for new forms of "banana wars" over genetic advantages, designer babies, and extended lifespans for the wealthy, creating deeper chasms of inequality. This isn't a divine curse or a punishment for sin; it's the cold, hard logic of a species operating on primal imperatives, masked by a fragile illusion, and armed with increasingly powerful tools.

To truly understand our future, we must look not to a moral compass we do not possess, but to the unvarnished reality of our amoral selves. The bonobo paradox showed us that even cooperation is a calculated strategy for more bananas; the ape-oca-lypse is simply the logical outcome when individual or tribal WI-IFM overrides the broader, more complex cooperative strategies needed for planetary survival. The fundamental challenge lies in the inherent conflict between short-term WIIFM (immediate profit, individual gain, tribal dominance) and long-term WIIFM (species survival, planetary viability). Our cognitive biases—optimism bias, confirmation bias, the illusion of control—and the seductive power of our narrative veils (Chapter 2, 4) blind us to the severity of this conflict. The question is not whether we are good enough to survive, for "goodness" is but a convenient construct. The question is whether our innate drive for self-preservation – the most fundamental, ancient WIIFM of all – can, by sheer, amoral calculation, find a way to override the short-term, destructive impulses of banana acquisition. Can we, the naked apes, collectively recognize that the ultimate "banana" is the continued existence of our species on a viable planet, before we strip the planetary tree bare and condemn ourselves to a future echoing the screams from the Forbidden Zone? The ultimate trap (Chapter 10) may well be the one we build for ourselves, an intelligent, efficient, amoral species cornering itself into self-destruction, an inevitable consequence of our unbound pursuit of all the bananas.

Chapter Fifteen

Living Without Illusions: Acceptance, Strategy, and the Amoral Way Forward.

Our journey began by observing a chimp stealing a banana, and in doing so, we embarked on an excavation of our own deepest, most uncomfortable truths. We've peeled back the layers of the Great Illusion, revealed the Narrative Veils that obscure our motivations, and confronted the primal imperatives driving our relentless pursuit of "bananas." This exploration has shown how tribal loyalties and sophisticated traps manifest in the cutthroat dance of politics and the insatiable void of wealth accumulation. We've even re-evaluated our cooperative instincts, finding them to be not moral virtues, but strategic tools for collective gain, born of environmental necessity rather than inherent goodness. And in the chilling Echoes of Ape-ocalypse, we glimpsed the logical, unvarnished consequences of our amoral trajectory, a future sculpted by the predictable intersection of boundless desire and finite resources.

Now, as the final curtain falls on these illusions, the concluding philosophical challenge presents itself: What does it truly mean for you, the reader, to accept this reality? This is not an invitation to despair, nor a license for unchecked nihilism or a descent into chaos. Instead, it is a call to profound clarity, a seismic shift in perspective that strips away comforting fictions and empowers you to navigate the world as it truly is, not as you wish it were. It means wielding truth as your ultimate tool, unburdened by the emotional and cognitive costs of delusion.

Acceptance is the first, most liberating step. To live without illusions is to acknowledge that human beings, including yourself, are fundamentally amoral creatures. Our inherent drives for dominance, security, reproduction, and resource acquisition aren't "good" or "bad"; they simply exist. They are the engine of our existence, meticulously shaped by millions of years of evolution, optimizing for survival and propagation. This stance, firmly rooted in a naturalistic worldview, directly challenges any notion of objective, inherent moral truths existing independently of our cognition. What we often label as "morality," we understand, is upon closer inspection a complex and highly effective set of strategic tools that have evolved to facilitate collective gain and individual survival. Some might accuse this view of being reductionist, simplifying the rich tapestry of human experience to mere biological impulses, ignoring the profound influence of culture, education, empathy, and conscious ethical deliberation. But our analysis suggests that even seemingly altruistic or compassionate behaviors can be reframed within this amoral framework as sophisticated, long-term, self-interested strategies for securing more "bananas." The point isn't to deny the existence of what we call kindness or virtue, but to understand their functional origins within the amoral game.

Releasing the burden of a falsely imposed morality allows you to see the true motivations behind actions, both your own and others', with a dispassionate, analytical gaze. You are no longer wrestling with perceived moral failures; you are observing the efficient, if sometimes brutal, mechanics of the banana game. This clarity is not a void; it is a foundation. It allows you to shed the costly burden of illusion—the emotional toll of constant disappointment when others don't live up to your imagined moral standards, the strategic disadvantage of being manipulated by appeals to non-existent virtues, and the personal frustration of self-flagellation over "immoral" desires that are simply innate drives. Much like the wisdom found in Stoic philosophy or the practical applications of cognitive behavioral therapy, accepting reality as it is—rather than as we wish it to be—paves the way for greater effectiveness. The "Finders Keepers, Losers Weepers" rule, a principle we've previously explored, applies to truth as well: those who grasp it first gain the advantage. Some might fear this liberation leads to cynicism or a cold, calculating detachment, fearing it strips humanity of its warmth and genuine connection. Yet, understanding the amoral drivers allows for a more resilient and authentic engagement with the world. Relationships built on transparent, mutual (albeit amoral) benefit are often more robust than those resting on fragile, easily shattered ideals, leading to more stable and predictable interactions. Emotions do not vanish, but by understanding their evolutionary function, you gain greater self-control and the ability to act more deliberately.

This unvarnished understanding, far from leading to a descent into chaos, provides the robust foundation for strategic navigation of human interactions and the broader world. If you recognize that every individual, every group, and every nation primarily operates from a place of self-interest in the relentless pursuit of their "bananas," then you gain immense tactical and predictive advantage. You can anticipate behaviors, understand underlying conflicts, and position yourself more effectively. This insight significantly enhances your agency in the world, allowing for conscious choices based on realistic assessments rather than unconscious drives masked by moral pretense. This approach aligns perfectly with game theory, where anticipating the self-interested moves of other players proves crucial for optimizing one's own strategy.

In personal interactions, for example, you can more effectively negotiate, forge genuine alliances, or defend your own "bananas" because you understand the underlying drivers of others' behaviors. You are less likely to be swayed by emotional appeals designed to exploit your ingrained, but ultimately false, moral programming. You can identify the traps others set, and set your own more effectively, always with an eye on the exchange of value. This clarity allows for relationships built on transparent, mutual, albeit amoral, benefit, rather than fragile, easily shattered ideals. Your actions become calculated, deliberate, and thus, more powerful. This isn't a call to ruthlessness, but to astute effectiveness, enabling you to build genuine rapport based on shared, understood interests.

In the political arena, rhetoric ceases to be about justice or righteousness and becomes a transparent competition for power and resources, thinly veiled by ideology. You become significantly less susceptible to propaganda and emotional manipulation, able to discern the true beneficiaries of policies and the strategic moves behind the public facade. This mirrors realist theories in international relations, where national interest and power are the ultimate arbiters. You recognize that every political maneuver is a calculated attempt to secure "bananas" for a specific group, and you can decide where your own self-interest truly lies, becoming a more discerning and effective participant or observer in the game of states. Understanding this amoral undercurrent empowers you to navigate the political landscape with eyes wide open.

In competitive industries and the economy, the "Unwritten Rule: Finders Keepers, Losers Weepers" transforms from a harsh truth into a clear operating principle. You can strategically position yourself for success, recognize exploitative practices without surprise, and protect your hoard without the cognitive dissonance of believing the game is inherently "fair." You learn to play the banana game more effectively, not because you are inherently "better," but because you are fundamentally more realistic. Some might contend this encourages ruthlessness, potentially dissolving social cohesion and trust. However, the framework argues that understanding the competitive landscape allows for self-preservation and the ability to identify truly beneficial, albeit amoral, collaborations, making your interactions more effective and less prone to naive disappointment. This isn't about being cruel; it's about being effective, understanding the true currents of trans-actional value.

Finally, regarding self-awareness, by recognizing your own amoral imperative, you gain an unprecedented degree of self-control and personal effectiveness. Your emotions—anger, jealousy, even what feels like "altruism"—can be seen not as moral compasses, but as evolved mechanisms designed to achieve amoral ends. This profound self-awareness allows for more deliberate, calculated choices, enabling you to pursue your own "bananas" with greater effectiveness and less internal conflict, even if those choices are still, at their core, amoral. You can leverage your own drives, rather than being blindly driven by them, achieving a new level of mastery over yourself. This self-mastery is perhaps the most profound personal outcome of living without illusions.

Crucially, this acceptance does not aim for "good." That concept, in its intrinsic sense, does not exist within this framework. The "way forward" is not a path to moral enlightenment, but a path to personal effectiveness, strategic success, and optimized survival in the complex, relentless "banana game." It is about achieving your own objectives, securing your own well-being, and thriving within the system as it truly operates. This framework, far from leading to nihilism, actually provides the only pragmatic basis for large-scale, collective action aimed at species-level self-preservation.

If cooperation is merely a strategy for more bananas, then understanding its mechanisms, as we have, allows us to design systems and incentives where individual WIIFM (What's In It For Me) aligns with the collective "ultimate banana" of shared survival. This is not "enlightened self-interest" in a fluffy, moral sense, but a cold, hard, amoral calculation: the most efficient way for you to secure your own long-term "bananas" might just be to ensure the survival of the planetary orchard itself. Some might raise concerns about this leading to the justification of any means to an end, fearing an ethical vacuum that could justify problematic actions. However, the counter-argument is deeply pragmatic: unchecked, short-sighted individual acquisition inevitably undermines the very resources necessary for anyone's long-term success. Species survival becomes the most rational, long-term self-interested goal for every individual within that species, making it a utilitarian calculus for the largest possible "good," framed purely as survival. This perspective offers a sober, yet potent, pathway for humanity's long-term prosperity.

To live without illusions is to embrace the formidable, cunning ape within. It is to acknowledge the truth of our nature, to shed the comforting fictions, and to wield this knowledge not for universal salvation, but for the clarity and strategic advantage it offers in navigating the only world that truly exists: an amoral one. The power, once hidden behind the veil, is now yours to command. The ultimate question isn't whether we can become "good," but whether our collective amoral shrewdness—the very capacity for strategic calculation that built our complex societies—can evolve to prioritize the largest, longest-term "banana" of species survival over the fleeting, destructive gains of individual acquisition. This knowledge, once accepted, is the only map we possess to navigate the treacherous path that leads either to the ultimate hoard of planetary devastation or, perhaps, to a pragmatic, effective, albeit entirely amoral, future.

Chapter Sixteen

The Awakened Ape: Crafting One's Path in an Amoral World

O ur journey has stripped away layers of comforting fiction, revealing the raw, amoral engine that drives human behavior. We've seen that our relentless pursuit of "bananas" stems not from virtue or vice, but from deep-seated evolutionary imperatives. Chapter 16 concluded by inviting you to accept this truth, offering clarity and strategic advantage in return for shedding the Great Illusion. Yet understanding alone is inert. The true challenge now emerges: What does it mean to live as an awakened ape, to apply this profound, often uncomfortable, knowledge to the intricate canvas of your daily existence? How does one craft a meaningful and effective path forward when the very concept of intrinsic "good" has been unmasked as a strategic construct, when the foundations of traditional morality seem to dissolve into a mere interplay of self-interest?

This final phase of our exploration moves from observation to action, from acceptance to agency. It's about building a personal philosophy, a set of operating principles that align with reality, not delusion. If the world is a game of "bananas"—a relentless, evolutionary drive for resources, security, and propagation—then the awakened ape, unburdened by false moral programming, possesses the unique opportunity to define their own desired outcomes with unprecedented clarity and pursue them with un-matched effectiveness. This isn't about becoming a selfish carica-ture, a detached sociopath; it's about optimizing your individual trajectory in a world fundamentally shaped by self-interest. Some might argue this framework is overly cynical, ignoring humanity's genuine capacity for empathy and altruism that so many humans display. However, the awakened ape doesn't deny the existence of these emotions, but understands their evolutionary function: they are complex adaptations that facilitate social cohesion and coop-eration, ultimately serving the long-term, collective self-interest of a highly social species.

The first, critical step in living as an awakened ape involves defining your "bananas." In the absence of an externally imposed moral compass, what truly drives you? For many, the immediate assumption might be crude wealth or brute power, and certain-ly, these are potent motivators, deeply ingrained in our primate heritage. But the pursuit of "bananas" extends far beyond simple acquisition. It encompasses a multifaceted array of deeply per-sonal and evolutionarily significant needs: the profound security of a stable home, the comfort of reliable resources, the intellectual challenge of mastery, the creative expression of art or innovation, the genuine connection within a trusted tribe, and the well-being of one's offspring or closest kin. An awakened ape recognizes that even seemingly altruistic drives, such as devoted parental care, communal defense, or contributing to a collective endeavor like scientific discovery, are ultimately rooted in the perpetuation of one's own genes, the security of one's environment, or the strategic advantages derived from a thriving group. When you volunteer for a cause, for example, it's not merely out of abstract goodness; it might be because a healthier community benefits your own well-being, enhances your social standing, or satisfies an evolved need for group affiliation. The liberation lies in ac-knowledging these underlying drivers without guilt or pretense. By understanding that your desires, whatever their form, are simply evolved imperatives, shaped over millennia to maximize survival and reproduction, you can pursue them with greater honesty and fewer internal conflicts. No longer will you battle "immoral" urges that are, in fact, biological predispositions; you'll understand them as aspects of your fundamental design, to be leveraged or strategically managed, not suppressed for an imagined virtue. Critics might suggest this approach reduces the richness of human motivation, stripping away genuine nobility, but it actually provides a clearer, more grounded foundation for self-understanding and deliberate action, allowing for a robust self-acceptance that traditional morality often denies.

With this clear-eyed self-awareness comes a distinct, formidable form of agency. You stop being a reactive player in the banana game, unconsciously manipulated by appeals to non-existent virtues or trapped by your own unexamined desires. Instead, your actions become calculated, deliberate. You choose your strategies based on realistic assessments of human nature, knowing that others, like you, are driven by their own pursuit of "bananas." This insight profoundly transforms interactions. Negotiations become clearer, focused on transparent exchanges of value, rather than veiled attempts at moral one-upmanship. If a business deal is mutually beneficial, it proceeds. If it is one-sided, you understand why the other party acts as they do and can adjust your strategy accordingly. Alliances, whether personal or professional, are forged not on brittle ideals of immutable loyalty, but on robust, mutual self-interest—a far stronger and more sustainable foundation. When you understand that trust is a strategic investment rather than an inherent moral obligation, you can build it meticulously where it serves your purpose, and conversely, protect yourself judiciously where it might be exploited. For instance, you might trust a colleague with a critical task not because they are "good," but because their "banana" (e.g., career advancement, reputation) aligns perfectly with the successful completion of the task, creating a powerful incentive for them to perform. This is the essence of wielding truth as your ultimate tool: anticipating behaviors, understanding hidden agendas, and positioning yourself to secure your own outcomes effectively. Some might see this approach as cold or even manipulative, stripping relationships of warmth. However, by removing the false pretense of pure altruism, it actually fosters a more honest and durable form of human connection, based on shared, transparent interests rather than fragile, easily shattered illusions.

Crafting a personal code in this amoral landscape is not about abandoning principles, but about building them on solid ground. Your principles become pragmatic choices for effective living, rather than aspirational, often unattainable, moral dictates. For instance, you might value honesty not because it is inherently "good," but because it fosters predictable interactions, builds strategic alliances based on reliability, and avoids the costly cognitive load and reputational damage of maintaining deception. Similarly, integrity becomes a highly valuable asset because it makes you a dependable partner in the banana game, attracting those whose self-interest aligns with yours. Cooperation remains not only essential but even more vital, yet it stems not from an abstract sense of duty, but because collective effort often yields a larger "ultimate banana" for everyone involved than individual striving could ever achieve. Consider global efforts to combat climate change: while moral arguments are made, the underlying amoral driver is the collective self-interest in preserving a habitable planet—a fundamental "banana" for all. Your actions are thus guided by what works for your long-term success and well-being, both individually and within your chosen tribal structures. This is a robust framework, one that does not shatter when faced with the harsh realities of human behavior or the inevitable disappointments that arise from expecting others to act against their own deepest drives. This system, far from leading to chaos, offers a pragmatic path to societal order and personal effectiveness.

The awakened ape finds solace not in naive optimism, which is so easily shattered by reality, but in profound realism. There is no moral high ground to fall from, only a clearer understanding of the terrain. This perspective empowers, rather than diminishes. It replaces the endless frustration of wishing people were "better"—a wish that fundamentally misunderstands human nature—with the practical challenge of understanding why they are exactly as they are, and then acting accordingly. The internal conflict that plagues so many—the struggle between innate desires and socially imposed moralities—dissolves into a unified, self-aware pursuit of chosen "bananas." This doesn't lead to isolation; paradoxically, it allows for more genuine connections. When you remove the pretense of pure, unconditional love or altruism, relationships can be built on acknowledged self-interest and transparent exchange, rather than veiled expectations and inevitable disappointment. You learn to appreciate acts of kindness not as proof of inherent goodness, but as sophisticated cooperative strategies that benefit both giver and receiver, making them no less valuable. The anxieties of moral judgment, both self-imposed and externally applied, diminish. This self-mastery, this profound clarity, is perhaps the most significant personal outcome of living without illusions. It's a challenging but ultimately liberating emotional landscape.

Ultimately, living as an awakened ape is about embracing the formidable, cunning intelligence that evolution has bestowed upon us. It's about shedding the comforting fictions that have historically constrained our agency and obscured our true motivations. The path forward is not paved with moral enlightenment, but with strategic clarity, pragmatic cooperation, and an unwavering commitment to securing your chosen "bananas" in the only world that truly exists: an amoral one. Your power, once hidden behind the veil, is now truly yours to command, offering a unique opportunity to shape your destiny and contribute to the collective survival of the planetary orchard itself, for that, too, is the largest, longest-term "banana" of all.

If cooperation is merely a strategy for more bananas, then understanding its mechanisms, as we have, allows us to design systems and incentives where individual WIIFM (What's In It For Me) aligns with the collective "ultimate banana" of shared survival. This is not "enlightened self-interest" in a fluffy, moral sense, but a cold, hard, amoral calculation: the most efficient way for you to secure your own long-term "bananas" might just be to ensure the survival of the planetary orchard itself. Some might raise concerns about this leading to the justification of any means to an end, fearing an ethical vacuum that could justify problematic actions. However, the counter-argument is deeply pragmatic: unchecked, short-sighted individual acquisition inevitably undermines the very resources necessary for anyone's long-term success. The pursuit of fleeting gains often leads to the destruction of the very environment that produces the "bananas." Species survival, therefore, becomes the most rational, long-term self-interested goal for every individual within that species, making it a utilitarian calculus for the largest possible "good," framed purely as survival. This perspective offers a sober, yet potent, pathway for humanity's long-term prosperity, grounding grand aspirations in the undeniable bedrock of biological reality.

To live without illusions is to embrace the formidable, cunning ape within. It is to acknowledge the truth of our nature, to shed the comforting fictions, and to wield this knowledge not for universal salvation, but for the clarity and strategic advantage it offers in navigating the only world that truly exists: an amoral one. The power, once hidden behind the veil, is now yours to command. The ultimate question isn't whether we can become "good," but whether our collective amoral shrewdness—the very capacity for strategic calculation that built our complex societies—can evolve to prioritize the largest, longest-term "banana" of species survival over the fleeting, destructive gains of individual acquisition. This knowledge, once accepted, is the only map we possess to navigate the treacherous path that leads either to the ultimate hoard of

planetary devastation or, perhaps, to a pragmatic, effective, albeit
entirely amoral, future.

Chapter Seventeen

Everyday Examples of Humans Stealing each other's Bananas.

T he Primate Principle asserts that beneath the veneer of morality and civility, humans are fundamentally driven by an amoral imperative to secure and hoard resources, or "bananas." This drive manifests not just in grand acts of conquest or corporate malfeasance, but in the subtle, often legal, everyday interactions that define our modern "Asphalt Jungle." What follows are just a few common examples, demonstrating how individuals and institutions, operating as "What's in It for Me?" machines, constantly seek to acquire their share of bananas from others, often by leveraging illusions, vulnerabilities, or systemic advantages.

The Illusion of the Discount: The Banana Always Cost the Same

Imagine you walk into a store, and a bright red sign screams, "50% OFF! LIMITED TIME ONLY!" Your primate brain, ever vigilant for a good deal – a quicker, easier path to the "banana" – lights up. This feels like an opportunity, a chance to acquire a resource with less effort. But is it? Sometimes, the "sale" is nothing more than a carefully constructed illusion. The item might have been marked up significantly just before the "sale" began, so the "discount" merely brings it back to its standard, everyday price. Or, perhaps, the "original" price was an artificially inflated "manufacturer's suggested retail price" that the item rarely, if ever, actually sold for. The price point remains constant, yet the perception is cleverly altered. This isn't about outright theft in the traditional sense; you're still paying for the item. However, it's a subtle form of "banana stealing" on the part of the seller. They are leveraging your innate drive for advantage – your desire to maximize your resources and minimize your effort – to convince you to make a purchase you might not otherwise have, or to feel a false sense of urgency and satisfaction. The "narrative veil" here is spun thin, a shimmering mirage of savings. The "amoral reckoning" reveals that the merchant isn't operating on a principle of fairness or generosity, but on a pragmatic understanding of human psychology: if they can make you feel like you're getting more for less, they secure their own "banana" (your money) with greater efficiency. You, the consumer, are simply an opportunity in their "jungle," a source of resources to be cleverly influenced. It's the modern equivalent of one ape distracting another with a shiny object while quietly snagging the juiciest fruit.

The Greasy Gambit: Metal Filings and the Phantom Problem

Beyond deceptive pricing, some "banana steals" exploit a lack of specialized knowledge to inflate costs. Your car is making a strange noise, or maybe it's just due for a routine check-up. You take it to the transmission shop, hoping for a simple fix. The mechanic, with a somber expression, emerges from under your vehicle, holding up a pan with a few shimmering flecks at the bottom. "See these," he says gravely, pointing to the tiny metallic particles, "metal filings. This means your transmission is eating itself alive. You're looking at a complete rebuild or a new unit – easily five thousand dollars." To the average car owner, this sounds catastrophic. The glint of metal, the technical jargon, the authoritative tone – it all triggers a primal fear of loss, of being stranded, of a major financial hit. Your "banana" (reliable transportation, financial security) is under threat.

Here's the "banana steal" at play: a certain amount of metal particulate in a transmission pan is normal. As gears mesh and components wear over tens of thousands of miles, tiny, almost microscopic shavings will inevitably collect on the drain plug's magnet. It's a sign of a working system, not necessarily a dying one. A truly failing transmission would have chunks, shards, or a pan full of sludge, not just a fine dusting. The "steal" isn't just the potential overcharge for an unnecessary repair; it's the exploitation of your ignorance and your instinctive desire to avoid greater harm. The mechanic, in this scenario, is acting as a predator who has identified an opportunity. They understand that by presenting a normal wear-and-tear byproduct as a critical failure, they can induce panic and secure a massive "banana" from your wallet. This is the "fine art of the trap" in action, a contemporary pitfall for the "naked ape." The "narrative veil" they weave is one of impending doom, obscuring the simpler, less profitable truth. It's a cold, amoral calculation: leverage fear, capitalize on asymmetry of information, and secure the "top banana." For the shop, your fear is just another path to more bananas.

The Vanishing Jobber: The Ultimate Banana Snatch

Sometimes, the "banana steal" isn't subtle; it's an outright vanishing act. Imagine you're embarking on a home renovation, a dream project, or a critical business upgrade. You hire a contractor, a "jobber," who seems professional and trustworthy. They present a reasonable quote, talk a good game, and then ask for a substantial upfront deposit – say, ten thousand dollars – to cover materials and initial labor. Your primate brain assesses the risk: this person promises to deliver a significant "banana" (a completed project, improved living or working conditions) and requires an investment to get there. It feels like a standard transaction. You hand over the money, perhaps even feel a sense of relief that things are moving forward. But then, the phone calls stop. Emails go unanswered. Work never begins. The "jobber" has vanished, taking your ten thousand dollars – your "banana" – with them.

This isn't a subtle illusion or a manipulation of perception; this is a clear, unadulterated theft of resources. The "jobber" leveraged your trust and your need for their service to acquire your "banana" directly, offering nothing in return. They operated entirely within the amoral framework of "finders keepers, losers weepers." They identified an opportunity (your desire for a service and your willingness to pay), set a trap (the deposit), and executed the "steal." In the "Asphalt Jungle," this is a classic example of predation. The "jobber" doesn't see you as a client with needs but as a source of "bananas" to be exploited. Their "dominance drive" manifests not through physical prowess, but through cunning and deceit. Your loss is their gain, a pure transfer of resources motivated by self-interest, with no moral compass to guide the transaction. It's a stark reminder that in an amoral world, some "apes" are simply better at securing "bananas" by any means necessary, even if it means leaving others empty-handed and bewildered.

The Perpetual "Sale": Manufactured Urgency and the Phantom Discount

Another variation of sales deception plays on urgency. Consider the high-end window company. They proudly announce three major "sales" a year: perhaps a Spring Savings Event, a Summer Refresh Sale, and a Winter Warmth Discount. Each time, the advertisements promise substantial savings, perhaps 20% off, or a "buy one, get one half off" deal. Then, to add a layer of pressure, they offer an additional "$500 discount if you purchase within 30 days," implying a special, fleeting opportunity. Your primate brain, attuned to scarcity and value, registers these as genuine opportunities. The "What's in It for Me?" machine whirs, calculating the perceived savings. You feel compelled to act quickly, lest you miss out on a prime "banana" acquisition.

The "steal" here is multi-layered and insidious because the discount is often an illusion. If you were to track their pricing, you'd discover that the "sale" price is, in reality, their standard operating price. The initial, higher price from which the discount is calculated is rarely, if ever, charged. Furthermore, the "$500 if you purchase within 30 days" is not a bonus, but a component already baked into that standard price. It's designed not to reward you, but to accelerate your decision-making and prevent you from shopping around. This isn't just a benign marketing tactic; it's a calculated exploitation of our psychological vulnerabilities. The company isn't operating from a place of generosity, offering genuine savings. Instead, they understand that by creating the perception of a discount and a time-limited offer, they can increase conversion rates, reduce decision fatigue, and ultimately secure their "banana" (your money) with greater efficiency. The "narrative veil" is spun thick with promises of freedom from utility bills and environmental heroism. But beneath the surface lies the "fine art of the trap," where the bait is "free," and the hook is a multi-decade financial obligation. For the "solar ape," your desire for a better, cheaper future is simply an opportunity to secure their own hoard, regardless of the true cost to your "bananas" in the long run.

The Californio Land Grab: When the "Deed" Became the Weapon

Moving from individual transactions to systemic acquisitions, history provides stark examples of "banana stealing." Imagine the Californios, the original Hispanic settlers of California, living on vast ranchos passed down through generations. Their claim to the land was based on Spanish and Mexican land grants, often recognized by custom, usage, and the physical boundaries they worked and lived within. Formal, paper deeds in the Anglo-American sense were often not a part of their legal tradition, or if they existed, were not easily translatable or understood by the new American legal system. Their "banana" was the land itself – their sustenance, their identity, their wealth.

With the American conquest of California after the Mexican-American War and the subsequent Treaty of Guadalupe Hidalgo, a new "tribe" arrived with a different set of "rules" for claiming and owning "bananas." The American legal system, driven by concepts of documented ownership, clashed head-on with the Californio way of life. The "steal" was initiated through a seemingly legitimate legal process. Despite the treaty promising to respect existing land rights, the 1851 Land Act created a commission requiring Californio landowners to prove their titles, often within a short timeframe and in English, with costly legal representation. This was an immense, often insurmountable, burden. Many Californios, unfamiliar with the new legal system, unable to afford lawyers, or lacking the specific forms of documentation demanded, found their claims rejected.

This was a systematic "banana steal" on a grand scale. The "new tribe" (the American settlers and legal system) used its dominant "toolkit" (Anglo-American law, surveying, and the power of conquest) to dispossess the "old tribe" (the Californios) of their most valuable resource. The "narrative veil" was woven around the concept of "legitimacy" and "proper ownership," obscuring the underlying amoral drive to acquire fertile land and rich resources for the surging American population. The "unwritten rule: finders keepers, losers weepers" was brutally enforced. The Californios lost their lands not because they weren't the original inhabitants or stewards, but because they lacked the specific, paper-based "proof" demanded by the more powerful, arriving "apes." It was the ultimate "original banana war" writ large, a conflict over resources where one side's "tradition" and "code" (the American legal system) completely overwhelmed and invalidated the other's, resulting in a massive transfer of "bananas" driven by pure, amoral self-interest and the dominance drive of the conquering force.

The "Free Solar" Fantasy: A Trojan Horse for Debt

Systemic "banana steals" often hide behind appealing promises. The eager solar salesperson knocks on your door or makes a slick presentation online. Their pitch is irresistible: "Get solar panels installed on your roof for free! Eliminate your electric bill! Save the planet!" It sounds like the ultimate "banana" – endless energy, no ongoing cost, and a virtuous contribution to the environment. Your innate drive to acquire resources for "free," to secure more with less effort, is immediately engaged.

Here's where the sophisticated "banana steal" unfolds. While the upfront installation cost might genuinely be $0, the "free" often hides a complex financial arrangement:

1. The Solar Lease: You don't own the panels. The solar company does. You effectively "rent" the panels, agreeing to a monthly payment for 20-25 years. This monthly payment is often designed to be slightly less than your current utility bill initially, creating the illusion of savings. However, these payments frequently include annual escalators (e.g., 2.9% increase per year), meaning your "free" solar becomes progressively more expensive over time, eroding or even eliminating future savings. The company, meanwhile, claims all the valuable federal tax credits and other incentives, which you would have received if you owned the system.

2. The Power Purchase Agreement (PPA): Similar to a lease, the company owns the panels. Instead of a fixed monthly rent, you pay for the electricity the panels produce at a set rate per kilowatt-hour. Again, this rate is initially pitched below grid electricity, but it often has an escalator. You're effectively buying electricity from a new, private utility that's built a small power plant on your roof, rather than your traditional utility. All incentives still go to the company.

3. The Zero-Down Loan: While you own the panels, the "no upfront cost" means you've taken out a substantial loan, often with a balloon payment tied to the federal tax credit. If you don't qualify for the full credit, or fail to claim it, you're hit with a massive,

unexpected payment. The loan itself might have high interest rates or fees bundled in, making the "free" installation far from it when the total cost over decades is considered.

This is the "What's in It for Me?" machine at its most deceptive. The solar company's amoral calculation is clear: leverage the widespread desire for savings and environmental consciousness. By masking long-term debt or rental obligations behind the alluring word "free," they secure their substantial "banana" (your contracted payments and the lucrative incentives) while offloading the perceived risk and long-term commitment onto you. The "narrative veil" is spun thick with promises of freedom from utility bills and environmental heroism. But beneath the surface lies the "fine art of the trap," where the bait is "free," and the hook is a multi-decade financial obligation. For the "solar ape," your desire for a better, cheaper future is simply an opportunity to secure their own hoard, regardless of the true cost to your "bananas" in the long run.

The Sales Manager's Shell Game: Adding Bananas to the Basket

Sometimes, a "banana steal" is sprung after you think you've secured a deal. You've done your research, negotiated fiercely with the salesperson, and finally landed on what you believe is a fair price for your new car – your ultimate "banana" of modern transportation. There's a handshake, a sense of relief, a moment where your primate brain thinks it has secured a great deal. Then, the salesperson says, "Great! Let me just take this to my sales manager for approval." This is where the "banana steal" often begins, the purposely misnamed sales manager is in fact a client manager. This person's real job isn't to approve your negotiated deal, but to strategically add costs, leveraging your emotional investment and fatigue.

The "steal" unfolds when the "client manager" returns, often with a seemingly benevolent smile, and tells you: "Okay, we can do this deal one of two ways..." What follows isn't a choice between genuinely different, equivalent options. Instead, it's a carefully constructed narrative designed to introduce a host of high-profit, low-value additions. They start with seemingly innocuous items: "Warranty" (not the factory warranty you already have, but often an extended, third-party warranty with questionable coverage and a massive markup), "Wax and Sealant" (a few hundred dollars for a quick application of products you could buy for twenty dollars and apply yourself), "Market Adjustment" (a completely arbitrary fee, often explained away by "high demand" or "supply chain issues," that simply inflates the price), and other items like "Fabric Protection," "VIN Etching," or "Nitrogen in Tires" – more high-margin add-ons, presented as essential for protecting your investment or enhancing your driving experience.

The "two ways to do the deal" is the "fine art of the trap" in action. One "way" might be slightly less expensive but still riddled with markups, while the other piles on even more. The goal isn't to give you a choice, but to make you feel like you're choosing between two valuable set of extras that were never part of your original negotiation. They're banking on your eagerness to finalize the purchase, your mental exhaustion from negotiating, and your desire to protect your "banana" (the new car) with seemingly beneficial additions. The "narrative veil" is spun with jargon ("market adjustment"), appeals to responsibility ("protect your investment"), and the illusion of choice. The "client manager" is the ultimate "What's in It for Me?" machine, meticulously trained to identify and exploit your post-negotiation vulnerability. This isn't about fair trade; it's about maximizing the "banana" extraction from a willing, if unsuspecting, participant. It's a prime example of "The Ultimate Hoard" – using influence and a pre-set system to "rip people off" legally and systematically.

The McKinsey Doctrine: Weaponizing Bureaucracy Against the Injured Ape

Beyond direct sales, some of the most profound "banana steals" are orchestrated at the corporate level, often with the help of top-tier consultants. Imagine you've paid your insurance premiums diligently for years, believing you're "in good hands" – that in a moment of crisis, your insurance company will be there to help you rebuild your life, your home, or your health. This is the promise, the implicit social contract, the ideal of cooperation within the modern human tribe. But then disaster strikes – a car accident, a house fire, a natural calamity. You file a claim, expecting your "banana" of protection to be delivered.

Instead, you encounter a brick wall, subtly constructed by design. This is where the unseen hand of powerful consulting firms like McKinsey & Company has played a pivotal role in the ultimate "banana steal" on a corporate scale. While they may not have explicitly admitted to telling insurers to "rip off customers," extensive investigations, court documents, and journalistic exposes have revealed how their strategies systematically aimed to minimize payouts and increase company profits, often at the direct expense of policyholders.

The core of their advice, often summarized as the "Three D's" – Deny, Delay, Defend – is a chillingly amoral strategy.

• Deny: Advise insurance adjusters to initially deny claims or offer significantly low "lowball" settlements, regardless of the claim's true value. The amoral calculation: a certain percentage of claimants, exhausted or desperate, will simply accept the reduced "banana" rather than fight.

• Delay: Implement processes that drag out the claims resolution. Lengthy investigations, endless paperwork, repeated requests for documentation, and slow communication. The amoral calculation: the longer it takes, the more frustrated and financially stressed the claimant becomes, increasing their likelihood of giving up or accepting a lower offer. Time, for the claimant, is a diminishing "banana."

• Defend: If a claimant refuses the low offer and seeks legal counsel, the advice is to aggressively "defend" the claim in court, even if the insurer knows its position is weak. The amoral calculation: litigation is expensive and time-consuming for the claimant; many lawyers will be deterred from taking on such cases, and many claimants will simply run out of resources or patience.

This is the "Ultimate Hoard" in action, refined by top-tier strategists. The insurance company, advised by consultants is only setting up an elaborate chimp trap, that isn't acting as a cooperative partner in a time of need; it's a "What's in It for Me?" machine, meticulously optimizing its processes to retain its massive "banana" hoard (premiums) and minimize its "banana" outflow (claim payouts). The "narrative veil" of being "in good hands" or a "trusted partner" is a cynical cover for a system designed to exploit vulnerability and asymmetric power. This example starkly reveals "The Bonobo Paradox" in a corporate context: Is cooperation just another path to more bananas? In the insurance industry, for many, the "cooperation" you extend through your premiums is weaponized against you. The system is rigged, not by outright illegal means in every instance, but by exploiting the legal and psychological loopholes of an amoral world to maximize the "bananas" for the powerful entity, leaving the individual policyholder feeling, quite literally, stripped of their rightful resources.

Prior Approval: The Bureaucratic Barrier to Your Bananas of Health

Similar to insurance claims, the healthcare system offers its own unique brand of "banana stealing." You have health insurance, perhaps one you pay dearly for, believing it's your safety net, your ultimate protection against the sudden, devastating loss of your "banana" of good health. Your doctor, a trained professional who understands your unique medical needs, prescribes a crucial medication, recommends a necessary scan, or schedules a vital procedure. You think, "Great, the path to healing is clear."

But then, the insurance company interjects with a demand for "prior approval," "prior authorization," or "pre-certification." This is a seemingly innocuous bureaucratic hurdle that is, in practice, a meticulously designed "banana steal." Ostensibly, prior approval is meant to ensure "medical necessity" and "cost-effectiveness." In reality, it functions as a powerful gatekeeping mechanism, often designed to deny, delay, and defend against payouts.

The "steal" occurs in multiple layers:

• Delay: Your doctor's office submits detailed paperwork, often requiring hours of administrative time, phone calls, and faxes (yes, faxes!). The insurance company then takes days, weeks, or even months to review, often asking for more information, delaying critical care. For patients with rapidly progressing conditions like cancer or serious infections, this delay can be catastrophic, leading to worsening health, greater suffering, and ultimately, more expensive (or even impossible) treatment down the line. Your "banana" of timely care spoils while the process grinds.

• Denial: Even after extensive documentation, the approval can be denied. The stated reasons might be vague, citing "not medically necessary," "experimental," or "not aligning with plan policy." These denials often come from reviewers who have never examined you, sometimes lacking the specific expertise of your treating physician. The amoral calculation is simple: a certain percentage of patients and doctors will give up after a denial, choosing a less effective or cheaper alternative, or simply forgoing care altogether. The insurance company retains its "banana" (your premium) without having to disburse a payout.

• Discouragement: The sheer administrative burden and the emotional toll of fighting for necessary care can be immense. Many patients, already ill or in pain, simply abandon the recommended treatment. Doctors report significant burnout due to the constant battles with insurers, pulling them away from direct patient care.

This is the "Ultimate Hoard" in the healthcare jungle, meticulously defended. The "narrative veil" is one of patient safety and cost control, but the underlying "What's in It for Me?" machine is ruthlessly efficient: maximize profits by minimizing expenditures. Health insurance companies, often influenced by external consultants aiming for greater "profitability" by reducing "leakage" (payouts), use prior authorization as a choke point. It's a chilling demonstration of "The Fine Art of the Trap," where bureaucracy is weaponized. Your expectation of protection is met with a labyrinth designed to exhaust your resources – your time, your energy, and ultimately, your health. For the insurance company, your medical need is simply an opportunity to exercise control, extract more administrative labor from providers, and ultimately, secure more of their own "bananas" by withholding yours.

The Convenient "Breakdown": Engineering Scarcity for Higher Bananas

Market manipulation provides another fertile ground for "banana stealing." Imagine driving to the gas station, ready to fill up your tank – your essential "banana" for mobility, work, and daily life. You notice the price has inexplicably jumped, sometimes dramatically. The news reports a "sudden, unexpected refinery breakdown" or "pipeline maintenance issues" in a faraway state. The narrative is spun: it's a genuine problem, an unavoidable disruption that just happens to lead to higher prices at the pump.

Here's the "banana steal" at play: While legitimate maintenance and unforeseen issues do occur, the convenient timing and frequency of these "breakdowns" or "maintenance events" often raise suspicion. Especially in regions prone to volatile gas prices (like California, where such events are frequently cited), these disruptions often coincide with periods of high demand, approaching holidays, or moments when market conditions are ripe for a price increase.

The "steal" isn't about physical theft, but about the manipulation of supply and demand through the creation or exaggeration of perceived scarcity. Gas companies, operating as "What's in It for Me?" machines, understand market psychology perfectly. When supply is perceived to be constrained, prices can soar. Even if the actual reduction in supply is minimal or temporary, the announcement of a "breakdown" creates immediate market anxiety and justifies price hikes that are often far greater than the actual cost impact of the disruption.

This is "The Fine Art of the Trap" applied on an industrial scale. The "narrative veil" is one of unavoidable circumstance and technical difficulties, masking a cynical, amoral calculation. The companies aren't acting out of altruism or even true necessity; they are seizing an opportunity to extract more "bananas" (your money) for the same product. They leverage your absolute need for their "banana" (fuel for your car) and the broader market's susceptibility to scarcity narratives. For the gas companies, a "breakdown" isn't just an operational hiccup; it can be a highly profitable event. It allows them to hoard their existing "bananas" (refined fuel) while simultaneously demanding a higher price for them from a desperate public. It's a powerful example of how "The Ultimate Hoard" is maintained and grown, not always through direct force, but through strategic manipulation of information and the exploitation of a captive market. In the amoral world of resource extraction, even a "broken" pipe can be a goldmine.

Bernie Madoff: The Grand Illusionist of Infinite Bananas

Perhaps the most infamous individual "banana steal" in recent memory is that of Bernie Madoff. For decades, Bernard Madoff cultivated an image of unparalleled financial genius, an exclusive oracle of investment returns. Wealthy individuals, charities, and institutions flocked to him, eager to gain access to his seemingly consistent, double-digit annual returns – returns that defied market fluctuations and seemed too good to be true, yet persisted year after year. The promise was simple: give Madoff your financial "bananas," and he would multiply them with an almost supernatural consistency.

This was the ultimate "narrative veil" woven by a single individual. Madoff wasn't investing in anything legitimate. Instead, he was running the largest Ponzi scheme in history. His strategy was brutally simple and amoral: use money from new investors to pay "returns" to older investors. There were no actual investments, no complex trading strategies, no real profits being generated. It was all a complete fabrication.

The "steal" was a slow, deliberate bleeding of resources, disguised by meticulously fabricated account statements and the illusion of success. Madoff built his trap on several primal human vulnerabilities:

• Trust and Exclusivity: Madoff cultivated an air of prestige and exclusivity, making it seem like a privilege to invest with him. People felt honored to be included, and this fostered a deep, often unquestioning trust. The "in-group" mentality, a tribal instinct, made victims less likely to question the source of their "bananas."

• The Lure of Consistent Returns: In a volatile financial world, Madoff offered steady, attractive returns that were high enough to be enticing but not so outlandish as to immediately trigger alarm bells. This consistency became its own powerful "narrative veil," making the scheme appear stable and legitimate.

• The Promise of Effortless Bananas: Investors simply handed over their capital, expecting it to grow with minimal effort or understanding on their part. This appealed to the fundamental "what's in It for Me?" drive, promising more "bananas" without the usual risks or complexities of real investment.

The collapse of Madoff's scheme during the 2008 financial crisis was inevitable. As the economy faltered, more investors sought to withdraw their money than Madoff could cover with new incoming funds. The entire fabricated edifice crumbled, revealing the billions in "paper wealth" that had never existed, and the actual losses of nearly $18 billion in investor capital. Bernie Madoff's case is a chilling testament to the pinnacle of individual "banana stealing." He didn't use physical force or overt coercion. Instead, he leveraged human psychology, trust, and the desire for effortless gain within an amoral framework. He saw people's savings not as sacred trusts, but as reservoirs of "bananas" to be siphoned off, demonstrating the ultimate "dominance drive" through intellectual cunning and a complete absence of moral constraint. For Madoff, the entire financial system was his personal "jungle," and his victims were merely opportunities to amass an unprecedented hoard.

The Political "Banana": Legislating Your Resources Away

Moving from individual fraud to the broadest systemic "banana steal," we turn to politics. Consider its very essence in an amoral world: it is the primary mechanism through which collective resources ("bananas" belonging to the entire tribe or nation) are allocated, redistributed, or concentrated. Every law passed, every tax levied, every regulation implemented, and every subsidy granted fundamentally shifts "bananas" from one group to another.

The "steal" in politics often isn't overt theft; it's the legalized, systematic redirection of public resources for private or narrow group benefit. This is the "Ultimate Hoard" being built through legislation.

Here's how it often plays out:

• The Lobbyist as Apex Predator: Powerful corporations, wealthy individuals, and special interest groups hire highly effective lobbyists. These aren't just polite advocates; they are skilled practitioners of the "Fine Art of the Trap." They spend millions on campaign contributions, lavish gifts, and persuasive arguments designed to influence politicians. Their "banana" is not just profit, but legislative advantage: tax loopholes, deregulation that cuts costs (regardless of public harm), favorable contracts, or policies

146

that stifle competition. The "bananas" they secure are ultimately diverted from public coffers or extracted from consumers and the environment.

• The "Revolving Door" Mechanism: Politicians and high-level bureaucrats often leave public service to work for the very industries they once regulated or legislated over. This "revolving door" is a direct pipeline for "banana stealing." Their intimate knowledge of the system and their personal connections allow them to secure enormous "bananas" (salaries, influence) for themselves, while their former public office provided the leverage to create policies beneficial to their future employers. It's the "What's in It for Me?" machine in its most blatant form, demonstrating how public service can be a strategic stepping stone to private gain.

• The Narrative Veil of "Public Good": The most insidious aspect of political "banana stealing" is the "narrative veil" woven to justify these actions. Tax breaks for corporations are spun as "job creation." Deregulation is pitched as "economic growth." Subsidies for specific industries are framed as "national security" or "innovation." Laws that favor powerful interests are presented as being for the "common good." This veil obscures the reality that these policies often concentrate "bananas" into the hands of a few, while the broader public bears the costs – whether through higher taxes, fewer public services, environmental degradation, or stifled competition.

Politics, in this light, is a relentless "Banana War" where different "tribes" (political parties, economic sectors, interest groups) battle for control over the collective "banana" supply. The politicians themselves become key gatekeepers and allocators, often driven by the "Dominance Drive" to accrue more power and influence, which in turn allows them to secure more "bananas" for themselves and their favored groups. It is the ultimate expression of an amoral reckoning, where the pursuit of power and resources dictates the rules of engagement, often leaving the average "ape" with a smaller share of the collective fruit.

The Politicized Gavel: Stealing the Banana of Impartial Justice

Following the broader discussion of how political systems redistribute "bananas," it's crucial to examine the more granular, yet equally impactful, arena of administrative law. Here, an insidious form of "banana stealing" occurs when the very arbiters of justice are compromised, undermining the promise of impartiality.

Imagine you are an individual appealing a government decision – perhaps a denial of disability benefits, a challenge to an environmental regulation impacting your property, or a dispute with a federal agency. You expect an Administrative Law Judge (ALJ) to hear your case fairly, objectively weighing the evidence according to the law. This expectation of impartiality is your "banana" of due process, the foundation of your trust in the system.

• The "Banana": Impartial judgment, fair hearing, due process, justice, the rightful claim or benefit you seek from a government agency.

• The "Stealer": Administrative Law Judges who are not truly independent but are connected to political factions or special interests, and the system that permits such connections to influence outcomes. For example, an ALJ freely admitted that he believes that employers should be allowed to fire anyone at any time. Suspiciously that judge is then given cases that peculiarly fall just in that realm. The trial is just a show so a box can be checked. At the end with no proof of transgression the judge has a way out. He is allowed to use his supposed "discretion" to decide. He will then speciously rule that he finds the petitioner is "truculent" or some other banana stealing techniques and does not deserve to have their job.

• The "Narrative Veil": The public trusts in the "independence" and "objectivity" of the judicial system, assuming that ALJs, like other judges, operate purely on legal merit. This veil promotes the idea of a level playing field, even when it's heavily tilted.

• The "Trap": Your reliance on the administrative process for justice, believing that the evidence will speak for itself. You are forced to present your case before an individual who may subtly (or overtly) favor the agency's position, a politically connected entity, or a specific ideological viewpoint.

• The "Steal": The "steal" occurs when an ALJ's decisions are influenced not by law or evidence, but by political considerations, personal bias, or connections to the very entities they are supposed to judge impartially. Your claim, your appeal, or your dispute is judged unfairly, leading to denial of benefits, imposition of penalties, or outcomes that favor powerful corporate or governmental interests over individual rights. These judges, acting as "What's in It for Me?" machines, might prioritize career advancement within a politically charged bureaucracy, appease influential patrons, or align with a particular agenda, thereby securing their own "bananas" (career stability, influence, favored status) at the expense of fair and equitable justice. This subversion of the judicial process is a profound "banana steal" because it erodes the public's faith in the fairness of the very institutions designed to protect their rights and allocate resources justly. It's a prime example of how "Dominance Drive" and the pursuit of "The Ultimate Hoard" can permeate even the supposedly neutral arbiters of legal decisions, leaving the "afflicted" without recourse. The petitioner was dead before the trial even started and is forced to sacrifice their bananas (money) for attorneys and filing fees.

The Divine Dividend: Trading Earthly Bananas for Heavenly Promises

Beyond the halls of power, ideological systems also provide fertile ground for "banana stealing." For countless generations, humans have sought meaning, community, and answers to the great mysteries of existence. Religions and cults often step into this void, offering a powerful "narrative veil" of cosmic purpose, salvation, re-incarnation or enlightened truth. The promise is often one of ultimate "bananas"—eternal bliss, spiritual awakening, or a privileged place in a chosen community. This promise appeals to our deepest desires for belonging and transcendence, offering relief from the existential dread of an amoral world.

Here's the "banana steal" at work:

The spiritual leader, prophet, or organization, acting as a supreme "What's in It for Me?" machine, recognizes that these profound human needs can be leveraged to acquire significant tangible "bananas." The transaction is often presented as a spiritual imperative, a pathway to the promised reward:

• Financial Contributions (Tithes & Offerings): Followers are encouraged, sometimes explicitly commanded, to donate a portion of their income or wealth, often under the guise of "sowing seeds for spiritual harvest," "supporting God's work," or "building the community." This is a direct transfer of financial "bananas," which then accumulate into the "Ultimate Hoard" of the religious institution or its leadership. The "narrative veil" here is that giving enriches the giver spiritually, even if it impoverishes them materially.

• Unpaid Labor and Property: Members might be required to dedicate vast amounts of unpaid labor to the organization, build structures, or even sign over personal property. This is a direct acquisition of physical "bananas" and time, justified by the "divine mandate" or the shared pursuit of a collective, often utopian, goal.

• Control and Autonomy: In more extreme cultic settings, the ultimate "banana" stolen is the individual's autonomy. Followers are encouraged to sever ties with outside family and friends, surrender decision-making power to the leader, and become completely dependent on the group for all their needs and beliefs. This allows the leader to amass absolute control, turning followers into obedient instruments for their own "Dominance Drive" and resource acquisition. The "flappers and the blind" often refuse to see that their agency is being systematically dismantled for someone's gain.

• The Illusion of Intangible Value: The "steal" is perpetuated by maintaining the illusion that the intangible spiritual benefits provided are worth the tangible sacrifices. The "Grand Illusion" is that morality, divine favor, or eternal life are conditional on adherence to the leader's commands and contributions to their "hoard."

In this amoral reckoning, the charismatic leader or manipulative institution sees the followers' hope, fear, and desire for meaning as a vast field of "bananas" to be harvested. The "narrative veil" provides justification, the "fine art of the trap" lies in the insidious erosion of critical thinking and external connections, and the "steal" culminates in the significant accumulation of wealth, power, and influence by those at the top, often at the profound expense of those who believed. It's a stark reminder that even the most sacred of human pursuits can become another pathway to acquiring "bananas."

The Phantom Publisher: Where Your Dreams Become Their Bananas

In the digital age, exploitation often targets aspirations. Imagine you're an aspiring author, brimming with the excitement of finally finishing your manuscript. Your "banana" is not just the book itself, but the dream of sharing your story, gaining recognition, and perhaps earning a living from your creative labor. You approach what seems like a legitimate "publishing company" you found online. Their website is slick, boasting American names and addresses in major U.S. cities. They promise a pathway to publication, marketing, and success.

Here's the "banana steal" that often unfolds:

You engage with their "representatives," often speaking with individuals who use Americanized names (but not their real names) They have distinct foreign accents usually Indian or Slavic. Despite their claimed U.S. presence, their operations are frequently based in other countries, leveraging VOIP phones to create a false sense of proximity. They have no verifiable physical address in the U.S.

and often operate in a legal gray area, evading taxes and account-ability in your jurisdiction. They also have no business certificate.

The "steal" comes in the form of hefty upfront fees for services that are either grossly overcharged, poorly executed, or entirely fictitious: editing, formatting, cover design, "marketing packages" costing $10,000 that yield zero results, and promises of distribu-tion that never materialize. They will tell you there is no guarantee it will work or take three years to materialize to cover their tracks when it doesn't. Your "banana" – your hard-earned money and the intellectual property of your book – is systematically siphoned away.

When you inevitably raise concerns about a lack of progress, the poor quality, the endless repeating of the same job yield-ing specious results the "narrative veil" twists. You're met with a litany of excuses: technical glitches, "unexpected delays," or the classic, infuriating blame game: "The person responsible for that no longer works here." This maneuver is designed to frustrate, confuse, and ultimately wear you down. The company, operating entirely as a "What's in It for Me?" machine, will then "bail out" – disappearing or ceasing communication – at the most opportune time for them, having extracted maximum "bananas" before any significant accountability can be levied. The concept of a starter and finisher now appears. The person who made the initial deal now disappears either finding another job, getting married or moving to another city, The second tier involves a person who actually produces some output. Now that you see some work and feel confident the finisher shows up. The big banana now arrives---the marketing package!! The fact that the person believes in themselves is used against them goading them on to sacrifice more "bananas" (money)

This is a meticulously constructed "trap" where the bait is the author's deepest aspiration. The "publishers" understand that creators are often desperate for a break, willing to invest in their dreams. Their amoral calculation is simple: create an elaborate illusion of legitimacy, collect fees, provide minimal or no valuable service, and then vanish or stonewall when challenged. It is the ultimate expression of "finders keepers, losers weepers," where your creative "banana" and financial investment are swallowed whole by a phantom entity, leaving you with nothing but a bitter taste and a broken dream.

The "I'm Your Friend, Here to Help" Ploy: Trust as a Path to Your Bananas

More intimate, yet no less devastating, is the "banana steal" that exploits personal trust. Imagine a situation where you are vulnerable: you're new to town, facing a difficult personal problem, struggling financially, or simply seeking genuine connection. Into this space steps someone who seems exceptionally kind, empathetic, and eager to assist. "Don't worry," they say with a warm smile, "I'm your friend, and I'm here to help." They offer advice, a shoulder to cry on, or even a seemingly generous gesture. Your primate brain, hardwired for social connection and aid within the tribe, registers this as a beneficial alliance, a source of support.

Here's the "banana steal" that then unfolds, often slowly and subtly:

The "friendship" or "help" is the meticulously crafted narrative veil, designed to disarm your natural defenses and cultivate trust. It's the initial bait in "the fine art of the trap." Once this trust is established, the manipulator, operating purely as a "What's in It for Me?" machine, begins to extract your "bananas."

This extraction can take many forms:

• Financial Exploitation: They might "borrow" money they never repay, ask you to co-sign loans, convince you to invest in their dubious schemes, or subtly steer you towards financial decisions that benefit them.

• Labor and Resources: They might perpetually ask for favors, free labor, use of your car or property without compensation, or consume your time and emotional energy without reciprocation.

• Information and Influence: They might gather sensitive information about you to use later for blackmail or leverage, or use your social connections and influence for their own advancement.

• Emotional Manipulation: In the most severe cases, they might isolate you from genuine support networks, fostering dependence and control, effectively stealing your autonomy and sense of self.

The underlying amoral calculation is chillingly simple: your vulnerability and your need for connection are simply opportunities. The manipulator sees your resources – your money, your kindness, your network, your emotional well-being – not as shared assets within a friendship, but as "bananas" to be acquired. They weaponize your trust, knowing that people are less guarded when they believe they are among allies. When the "friendship" eventually collapses under the weight of one-sided demands, manipulation, or outright betrayal, you are left not only without your "bananas," but with the profound sting of violated trust. It's a stark reminder that in an amoral world, the "Dominance Drive" can manifest not through overt aggression, but through the insidious manipulation of human connection, turning the very desire for companionship into a vulnerability to be exploited for personal gain.

The Bait and Switch: Luring You In for a Different Banana

Often, deception is deployed to get you through the door for a less-than-advertised "banana." Imagine you're searching for a specific, desirable "banana"—perhaps a brand-new, high-definition television advertised at an unbelievably low price, or a car with a set of features you desperately want, priced well below the competition. The advertisement screams "Limited Stock!" or "Special Offer!" Your primate brain, ever keen to secure a valuable resource with minimal effort or cost, is immediately drawn in. This advertised item is the "bait." You rush to the store, or the dealership, excited by the prospect of snagging this incredible deal. You've invested your time, your hopes, and your mental energy into acquiring that specific banana.

Here's the "steal" that unfolds:

Upon arrival, you're met with disappointment. The advertised item is "just sold out," or "there was a mistake in the ad," or "that model doesn't come with the features you actually need." The "bait" is gone. However, the salesperson, operating as a "What's in It for Me?" machine, quickly pivots. "But," they say, "we have this model, which is much better for your needs, only slightly more expensive..." or "We can order that one for you, but it will take weeks, and this one is available now, and it's a newer model..." This is the "switch."

The trick is that the original "bait" was never truly intended for sale or was only available in such minuscule quantities as to be virtually unobtainable. Its sole purpose was to get you through the door, to overcome your initial inertia, and to create an emotional commitment to the purchase process. Once you're physically there, once you've invested your time and energy, you're less likely to walk away empty-handed. The "narrative veil" here is the initial promise of an incredible deal, masking the true intention: to sell you a different, often more expensive or higher-profit-margin "banana." The "fine art of the trap" lies in exploiting your desire for the initial lure and then leveraging your sunk cost (time, travel, emotional investment) to guide you towards a less favorable but ultimately more profitable transaction for the seller. It's an amoral calculation: manipulate desire, create commitment, and redirect the customer to a different "banana" that primarily benefits the "stealer," regardless of the customer's initial intent or best interest.

False Narratives: Weaving the Illusion to Steal Your Bananas

More fundamentally, many "banana steals" are orchestrated through the manipulation of truth itself. Imagine a powerful entity – a corporation, a political faction, or a well-funded advocacy group – that desires a specific "banana": perhaps a lucrative government contract, a favorable change in legislation, or public approval for a controversial product. Directly demanding these "bananas" might provoke resistance or expose their self-interest. So, they deploy the ultimate weapon: the false narrative.

A false narrative is a fabricated or heavily distorted story, meticulously crafted and relentlessly propagated, designed to manipulate public perception, trigger emotional responses, and guide behavior in a way that ultimately benefits the architects of the narrative. It's the most sophisticated "narrative veil," spun not just around a single transaction, but around an entire worldview.

Here's how this "steal" manifests:

• Manufacturing Consent for "Bananas": A corporation might relentlessly push the narrative that a certain regulation is "crippling innovation" or "killing jobs," even if internal data shows otherwise. The truth is, the regulation might simply be reducing their profit margins or requiring them to invest in safer, more environmentally friendly (and thus more costly) practices. The "banana" they seek is deregulation, which translates directly to increased profits at the expense of public safety or environmental health. The false narrative makes this "steal" seem like a necessary, even patriotic, act.

• Creating Crisis for Political Gain: A political faction might amplify or even invent a "crisis" – a supposed surge in crime, an existential threat from an external enemy, or an impending economic collapse – to justify policies that consolidate their power or divert public funds. The "banana" here could be increased military spending, a draconian new law, or a shift in public sentiment that secures electoral victories. The fear and urgency generated by the false narrative override rational debate, allowing the "stealers" to secure their desired "bananas" unchallenged.

• Shifting Blame and Evading Accountability: When faced with their own failures or misdeeds, powerful entities often deploy false narratives to deflect blame. They might invent a scapegoat

– "it's the fault of foreign competitors," "bad actors within a small group," or "the previous administration's policies" – even if their own actions are clearly at fault. The "banana" preserved here is their reputation, their continued access to resources, and their freedom from accountability, all protected by a cleverly constructed fictional reality.

This is the ultimate "Fine Art of the Trap," played on the grand stage of public consciousness. The creators of false narratives understand that humans are storytelling creatures, often preferring a simple, compelling story over complex, inconvenient truths. They exploit the "flappers and the blind," who are either unwilling or unable to pierce through the illusion. In an amoral world, the ability to control the story, to shape collective perception, is the most powerful tool for securing and hoarding "bananas" from the unsuspecting masses, proving that the greatest "steals" are often orchestrated not with force, but with fiction.

"Comfort the Afflicted, Afflict the Comfortable": The Media Mogul's Narrative Steal

This quote, often attributed to media magnate William Randolph Hearst, offers a fascinating lens through which to view "banana stealing," particularly under "The Narrative Veil: How We Weave Stories to Justify the Steal," and "The Ultimate Hoard: Politics, Influence, and Ripping People Off." While seemingly a moral declaration, in an amoral world, it reveals a sophisticated strategy for acquiring power and resources. On its surface, "Comfort the afflicted, and afflict the comfortable" sounds like a noble journalistic credo, a promise to champion the underdog and challenge the powerful. It paints the media outlet, or the politician, as a force for justice, an ally of the common person against the elite. This is the narrative veil, spun with a moralistic sheen, designed to win public trust and loyalty. Your primate brain responds positively to a perceived protector of the "tribe's" weaker members and a challenger to those who hoard "bananas" unfairly.

Here's how this seemingly altruistic slogan can become a pow-erful instrument for "banana stealing":

The "steal" isn't about physical resources directly taken from the public. Instead, it's about the acquisition of influence, public opinion, political leverage, and advertising revenue – all incredibly valuable "bananas" for a media empire or political faction.

1. "Comfort the Afflicted" (The Bait): By championing populist causes, sensationalizing stories of injustice, and focusing on the struggles of the "common person," the media outlet builds a loyal readership or viewership. They provide a sense of validation and outrage, making the "afflicted" feel seen and heard. This creates a strong emotional bond and a perception of shared values, turning the audience into a valuable "banana" themselves – a captive market, a voting bloc, or a source of sustained attention. The ".comfort" is a psychological reward that secures loyalty.

2. "Afflict the Comfortable" (The Attack, or The Diversion): The media then uses this built-up credibility to target the "comfort-able"—often established institutions, rival politicians, or com-peting businesses. This "affliction" might indeed expose genuine wrongdoing, but it can also be a strategic attack driven by self-in-terest. For instance, "afflicting" a wealthy rival could weaken their political influence, remove a business competitor, or simply gen-erate more sensational headlines that drive up readership and advertising profits. It also solidifies the perception that the media outlet is a fearless champion of the people, further enhancing its "banana" of influence.

This strategy is the "What's in It for Me?" machine operating on a grand scale. The media mogul or political actor isn't primarily driven by a genuine moral imperative. Instead, they understand that by strategically positioning themselves as champions of jus-tice, they can:

• Monopolize Narrative: Control the stories people believe, shaping public opinion to their advantage.

• Generate Revenue: Sensationalism sells newspapers, drives clicks, and attracts advertisers.

• Exert Political Power: By swaying public sentiment, they can make or break political careers, push legislation, and ultimately influence who controls the nation's biggest "banana hoards."

The phrase itself becomes the ultimate "narrative veil," cloaking a ruthless pursuit of influence and profit. It's a prime example of how even seemingly noble declarations can be weaponized in an amoral world, where the perception of doing good is simply another highly effective path to securing one's own "bananas."

Spam Telephone Calls: The Relentless Pursuit of Your Bananas

Moving to the more common, yet equally persistent, forms of direct "banana stealing," we encounter the relentless assault of spam telephone calls. Your phone rings. It could be a scam about:

• "Your Social Security number has been suspended!"
• "The IRS is calling about your arrest warrant for unpaid taxes!"
• "Your grandchild is in jail and needs bail money now!"
• "Your computer has a critical virus, and we're from Microsoft support."
• "You've won a lottery you didn't enter, just pay a small fee!"
• "Your car warranty is about to expire!"
• "Your utility service will be shut off in thirty minutes!"
• "We're calling about your credit card's high interest rates."

Each of these is a meticulously crafted "narrative veil," designed to trigger a specific emotion or perceived vulnerability to trick you into surrendering your "bananas." The calls are volume plays, pure amoral calculations that understand if they make enough calls, a certain percentage of "apes" will fall into the trap.

Let's look at a couple of common types:

1. The Impersonation Scare: Leveraging Fear and Authority (e.g., SSN or IRS Scams)

The phone rings, and an automated voice or a stern human voice declares, "This is the Social Security Administration. Your

Social Security number has been compromised and will be sus-pended if you don't press 1 immediately." Or, "This is the IRS. You owe back taxes, and a warrant has been issued for your arrest."

• The "Banana": Your money, your personal identity, your peace of mind.

• The "Narrative Veil": The impersonation of a legitimate, pow-erful authority (government, law enforcement) combined with an immediate, dire threat. This creates intense fear, bypassing ratio-nal thought.

• The "Trap": The demand for immediate action, often involving wire transfers, gift cards, or sharing sensitive personal informa-tion, all under the guise of "resolving" the fabricated crisis. You're told you can avoid arrest or save your identity by surrendering your "bananas."

• The "Steal": Your money is wired away, often untraceably, or your identity is stolen for future financial exploitation. For the scammer, your panic is simply an opportunity to secure their "hoard."

2. The Tech Support Hustle: Exploiting Ignorance and Trust

"Hello, this is Microsoft technical support. We've detected criti-cal viruses on your computer that are actively compromising your data." The caller sounds professional, authoritative, and helpful.

• The "Banana": Your money (for unnecessary "fixes"), remote access to your computer (for further exploitation), your personal data.

• The "Narrative Veil": The illusion of legitimate tech support, playing on a common fear of computer problems and a lack of technical expertise. The scammer pretends to be "comforting the afflicted" (you, with your "broken" computer).

• The "Trap": They guide you to download remote access soft-ware, allowing them to take over your screen. They then run fake scans, show you alarming but meaningless error messages, and claim to "fix" non-existent problems for hundreds or even thousands of dollars. They might even install malware or steal your personal files during the process.

• The "Steal": You pay for services you don't need, your computer is potentially compromised, and your data is at risk. For the scammer, your digital illiteracy and desire for help are just open pathways to your "bananas."

In both cases, these spam calls are relentless reminders that in an amoral world, the pursuit of "bananas" extends to every channel, exploiting every human vulnerability—fear, hope, ignorance, love for family, desire for a deal—with a cold, calculated efficiency. The "unwritten rule: finders keepers, losers weepers" is never more brutally enforced than when the phone hangs up, and your "bananas" are gone, leaving you with nothing but the echo of a false promise.

Wage Theft: Stealing the Bananas of Your Labor

Beyond consumer scams, the workplace itself can be a site of significant "banana stealing." You go to work every day, dedicating your time, skill, and effort. You believe you're trading your labor for an agreed-upon wage – a fair exchange for your "banana" of time and energy. However, for many workers, the "banana" is systematically diminished or outright stolen.

• The "Banana": Your earned wages, overtime pay, benefits, and even the value of your breaks.

• The "Stealer": Unscrupulous employers.

• The "Narrative Veil": Employers might tell you to "punch out, but keep working," to be a "team player," or to take on "salaried" duties that magically exempt them from overtime, even if your job doesn't legally qualify. They might misclassify you as an "independent contractor" to avoid paying taxes, benefits, or minimum wage. The narrative is often about "flexibility" or "building character," masking the actual theft.

• The "Trap": Your fear of losing your job, your desire for promotion, or simply your lack of knowledge about labor laws. You're made to feel that complaining will cost you even more "bananas" in the long run.

• The "Steal": This manifests as unpaid overtime, forced off-the-clock work, illegal deductions from paychecks, denial of legally mandated breaks, or being paid less than minimum wage. The employer, operating as a pure "What's in It for Me?" machine, recognizes that your labor is a valuable "banana," and any portion they can acquire without paying for it directly boosts their "hoard." It's a fundamental "finders keepers, losers weepers" applied to the most basic human resource: time and effort.

Planned Obsolescence: Engineering Your Bananas to Spoil

Even the products we buy are often part of a subtle "banana steal." You buy a new smartphone, a printer, or a washing machine. You expect it to last a reasonable amount of time, providing a consistent "banana" of utility. Yet, often within a few years – sometimes even sooner – the device inexplicably slows down, stops working effectively, or becomes impossible to repair.

• The "Banana": Your money spent on the product, the continued utility of the product, and ultimately, your freedom to not spend more.

• The "Stealer": Manufacturers, often in the tech or appliance industries.

• The "Narrative Veil": The marketing narrative is all about "innovation," "new features," and the constant push for "upgrades." You're led to believe that your old device is simply outdated, rather than designed to fail. Software updates might even be released that intentionally slow down older models, framed as "improvements."

• The "Trap": Products are designed with non-replaceable batteries, proprietary screws, glued-together components, or software that makes older models incompatible with new services. Repair becomes prohibitively expensive or impossible, forcing you into a repurchase cycle.

• The "Steal": Your initial investment is cut short. You are compelled to buy a new product sooner than necessary, providing a continuous flow of "bananas" to the manufacturer. This isn't about creating truly better products; it's about artificially limiting the lifespan of a "banana" you've already acquired, forcing you to acquire another one, ensuring the "What's in It for Me?" machine continues to churn out profits. It's an amoral calculation that prioritizes the producer's constant revenue stream over the consumer's long-term value or environmental sustainability.

Predatory Lending: Harvesting Bananas from Desperation

When life deals a tough hand, some entities are poised to "steal bananas" from your vulnerability. Imagine you're facing an unexpected financial emergency – a car repair, a medical bill, or a sudden job loss. Your immediate "banana" is cash, and you need it fast. Traditional banks might not lend to you, or their process is too slow. Then, you see an advertisement for a "payday loan" or "title loan" company, promising quick cash with "no credit check." They seem like a friendly lifeline, offering to "help" you out of a tough spot.

• The "Banana": Your immediate need for cash, and ultimately, your long-term financial stability and assets (like your car title or future wages).

• The "Stealer": Predatory lenders.

• The "Narrative Veil": The companies present themselves as solutions for emergencies, offering "fast cash" and "easy approvals." They focus on the convenience and immediate relief, obscuring the devastating long-term costs. The narrative is one of "helping" the underserved, when in reality they are exploiting vulnerability.

• The "Trap": The trap is sprung when you sign the loan agreement. What initially seems like a small loan quickly balloons due to exorbitant interest rates (often annual percentage rates of 400% or more), hidden fees, and short repayment terms. When you can't pay back the full amount by the next payday, the loan "rolls over," incurring more fees and interest, trapping you in a cycle of debt. If it's a title loan, your car becomes collateral, often repossessed for a small default.

• The "Steal": The lender systematically drains your "bananas." They profit immensely from your desperation, extracting far more than the original loan amount, often leaving you in a worse financial state than when you started. Your immediate need for cash is simply an opportunity for them to secure a disproportionately large hoard of your future earnings or assets. It's an amoral calculus where the profit motive ruthlessly preys on financial distress.

Subscription Traps & Dark Patterns: The Invisible Hand Taking Your Bananas

Finally, in our increasingly digital world, new forms of "banana stealing" have emerged. Many of our "bananas"—from entertainment to fitness to productivity tools—come via subscriptions. You sign up for a "free trial" or a low introductory offer, eager to access a new service. The process is smooth, quick, and convenient.

• The "Banana": Your money (monthly fees), your time (spent trying to cancel), your attention (through unwanted communications).

• The "Stealer": Companies designing deceptive online interfaces and subscription models.

• The "Narrative Veil": They promote the ease of signing up, the "flexibility" of monthly plans, and the "benefit" of a "free trial." They often highlight introductory offers without clearly disclosing the higher price after the trial or making cancellation terms obvious.

• The "Trap": This is where "dark patterns" come into play – interface designs specifically engineered to trick you into doing things you wouldn't otherwise do.

o "Roach Motel": It's easy to sign up, but incredibly difficult to cancel. The cancellation button might be hidden deep in menus, require multiple clicks through confusing pages, or force you to call customer service during limited hours.

o "Forced Continuity": After a free trial, your credit card is automatically charged for the full subscription without sufficient warning or easy opt-out.

o "Confirmshaming": When you try to decline an offer, the option to decline is worded in a way that shames you (e.g., "No thanks, I don't want to save money").

• The "Steal": You end up paying for months, or even years, for services you no longer use or never intended to purchase beyond the trial. Your efforts to unsubscribe are thwarted by intentionally convoluted processes. The companies accrue vast "bananas" through passive, often unnoticed, charges. Their "What's in It for Me?" machine understands that inertia, forgetfulness, and frustration are powerful tools. By making the path to cancel arduous, they continue to siphon off your "bananas" even after your desire for the service has vanished. It's a subtle but pervasive form of digital predation in our increasingly online world.

These myriad examples, from the grand historical land grabs to the minute tactics of a digital subscription, illustrate a singular, pervasive truth: human interaction, when stripped of its comforting illusions, is often a continuous negotiation and acquisition of resources. The pursuit of "bananas" is not an exception to "The Human Experience"; it is, in many ways, the very engine of our everyday lives.

Chapter One

De Waal, Frans. Chimpanzee Politics: Power and Sex Among Apes. Johns Hopkins University Press, 2007.

Morris, Desmond. The Naked Ape: A Zoologist's Study of the Human Animal. McGraw-Hill, 1967.

Swift, Jonathan. Gulliver's Travels. 1726.

Chapter Two

Nietzsche, Friedrich. Beyond Good and Evil: Prelude to a Philosophy of the Future. 1886.

Dawkins, Richard. The Selfish Gene. Oxford University Press, 1976.

Joyce, Richard. The Evolution of Morality. MIT Press, 2006.

Harari, Yuval Noah. Sapiens: A Brief History of Humankind. Harper, 2015.

Chapter Three

Cialdini, Robert B. Influence: The Psychology of Persuasion. HarperCollins, 2006.

Dawkins, Richard. The Selfish Gene. Oxford University Press, 2016.

De Waal, Frans. Chimpanzee Politics: Power and Sex Among Apes. Johns Hopkins University Press, 2007.

Hobbes, Thomas. Leviathan. Edited by J. C. A. Gaskin, Oxford University Press, 1998.

Kahneman, Daniel. Thinking, Fast and Slow. Farrar, Straus and Giroux, 2011.

Machiavelli, Niccolò. The Prince. Translated by George Bull, Penguin Books, 2003.

Morgenthau, Hans J. Politics Among Nations: The Struggle for Power and Peace. Knopf, 1985.

Swift, Jonathan. Gulliver's Travels. Edited by Claude Rawson, Oxford University Press, 2005.

Trivers, Robert. Natural Selection and Social Theory: Selected Papers of Robert Trivers. Oxford University Press, 2002.

Chapter Four

Chomsky, Noam. Manufacturing Consent: The Political Economy of the Mass Media. Pantheon Books, 1988.

Foucault, Michel. Discipline and Punish: The Birth of the Prison. Pantheon Books, 1977.

Harari, Yuval Noah. Sapiens: A Brief History of Humankind. Harper, 2015.

Arendt, Hannah. The Origins of Totalitarianism. Harcourt Brace Jovanovich, 1951.

Zimbardo, Philip G. The Lucifer Effect: Understanding How Good People Turn Evil. Random House, 2007.

Lifton, Robert Jay. Thought Reform and the Psychology of Totalism: A Study of "Brainwashing" in China. W. W. Norton & Company, 1961

Chapter Five

Cialdini, Robert B. Influence: The Psychology of Persuasion. HarperCollins, 2006.

Dawkins, Richard. The Selfish Gene. Oxford University Press, 2016.

De Waal, Frans. Chimpanzee Politics: Power and Sex Among Apes. Johns Hopkins University Press, 2007.

Harari, Yuval Noah. Sapiens: A Brief History of Humankind. Harper, 2015.

Hobbes, Thomas. Leviathan. Edited by J. C. A. Gaskin, Oxford University Press, 1998.

Kahneman, Daniel. Thinking, Fast and Slow. Farrar, Straus and Giroux, 2011.

Machiavelli, Niccolò. The Prince. Translated by George Bull, Penguin Books, 2003.

Morgenthau, Hans J. Politics Among Nations: The Struggle for Power and Peace. Knopf, 1985.

Pinker, Steven. The Blank Slate: The Modern Denial of Human Nature. Penguin Books, 2003.

Sapolsky, Robert M. Behave: The Biology of Humans at Our Best and Worst. Penguin Press, 2017.

Swift, Jonathan. Gulliver's Travels. Edited by Claude Rawson, Oxford University Press, 2005.

Tajfel, Henri, and John C. Turner. "The Social Identity Theory of Intergroup Behavior." The Psychology of Intergroup Relations, edited by Stephen Worchel and William G. Austin, 2nd ed., Nelson-Hall, 1986, pp. 7-24.

Trivers, Robert. Natural Selection and Social Theory: Selected Papers of Robert Trivers. Oxford University Press, 2002.

Chapter Six

De Waal, Frans. Chimpanzee Politics: Power and Sex Among Apes. Johns Hopkins University Press, 2007.

De Waal, Frans. Our Inner Ape: A Leading Primatologist Explains Why We Are Who We Are. Riverhead Books, 2005.

Ellis, Lee, et al. Sex, Status, and Aggression: A Biosocial Perspective. Birkhäuser, 2008.

Goleman, Daniel. Social Intelligence: The New Science of Human Relationships. Bantam Books, 2006.

Hrdy, Sarah Blaffer. Mother Nature: Maternal Instincts and How They Shape the Human Species. Ballantine Books, 1999.

Lomborg, Bjørn. The Skeptical Environmentalist: Measuring the Real State of the World. Cambridge University Press, 2001.

Marmot, Michael. The Status Syndrome: How Social Standing Affects Our Health and Longevity. Times Books, 2004.

Pinker, Steven. The Blank Slate: The Modern Denial of Human Nature. Penguin Books, 2002. Sapolsky, Robert M.. A Primate's Memoir: A Neuroscientist's Unconventional Life Among the Baboons. Scribner, 2001.

Sapolsky, Robert M.. Behave: The Biology of Humans at Our Best and Worst. Penguin Press, 2017.

Wilson, Edward O.. Sociobiology: The New Synthesis. Harvard University Press, 1975.

Dabbs, James M., and Robin Morris. "Testosterone, Social Class, and Antisocial Behavior in a Sample of 4,462 Men." Psychological Science, vol. 6, no. 4, 1995, pp. 209-11.

Denson, Thomas F., et al. "The Effects of Testosterone Administration on Aggression, Impulsivity, and Risk-Taking: A Meta-Analysis." Psychological Bulletin, vol. 143, no. 12, 2017, pp. 1243–76.

Frank, Robert H.. Success and Luck: Good Fortune and the Myth of Meritocracy. Princeton University Press, 2016.

Mazur, Allan, and Alan Booth. "Testosterone and Dominance in Men." Behavioral and Brain Sciences, vol. 10, no. 3, 1998, pp. 165-97.

Popa, Roxana. "Neurobiology of Social Hierarchy." Current Opinion in Neurobiology, vol. 61, 2020, pp. 110-16.

Sherman, Paul W., and John Alcock, editors. Explorations in Animal Behavior: Readings from American Scientist. Sinauer Associates, 1997.

Zink, Charles F., et al. "Dopaminergic Striatal Responses to Social Status." Neuron, vol. 48, no. 2, 2005, pp. 343-52.

Cole, Steven W.. "Social Regulation of Gene Expression in Human Leukocytes." Genome Biology, vol. 11, no. 6, 2010, p. 206.

Chapter Seven

Axelrod, Robert. The Evolution of Cooperation. Basic Books, 1984

Boyd, Robert, and Peter J. Richerson. The Origin and Evolution of Cultures. Oxford University Press, 2005

De Waal, Frans. Good Natured: The Origins of Right and Wrong in Humans and Other Animals. Harvard University Press, 1996

De Waal, Frans. The Bonobo and the Atheist: In Search of Humanism Among the Primates. W. W. Norton & Company, 2013

Harari, Yuval Noah. Sapiens: A Brief History of Humankind. Harper, 2015

Morris, Desmond. The Naked Ape: A Zoologist's Study of the Human Animal. Dell Publishing, 1967

Nowak, Martin A. Evolutionary Dynamics: Exploring the Equations of Life. Belknap Press of Harvard University Press, 200

Pinker, Steven. The Blank Slate: The Modern Denial of Human Nature. Viking, 2002

Shubin, Neil. Your Inner Fish: A Journey into the 3.5-Billion-Year History of the Human Body. Pantheon Books, 2008

Wright, Robert. The Moral Animal: Why We Are the Way We Are: The New Science of Evolutionary Psychology. Vintage Books, 1994

Chapter Eight

Axelrod, Robert. The Evolution of Cooperation. Basic Books, 1984

Boyd, Robert, and Peter J. Richerson. The Origin and Evolution of Cultures. Oxford University Press, 2005

De Waal, Frans. Good Natured: The Origins of Right and Wrong in Humans and Other Animals. Harvard University Press, 1996

De Waal, Frans. The Bonobo and the Atheist: In Search of Humanism Among the Primates. W. W. Norton & Company, 2013

Harari, Yuval Noah. Sapiens: A Brief History of Humankind. Harper, 2015

Morris, Desmond. The Naked Ape: A Zoologist's Study of the Human Animal. Dell Publishing, 1967

Nowak, Martin A. Evolutionary Dynamics: Exploring the Equations of Life. Belknap Press of Harvard University Press, 2006

Pinker, Steven. The Blank Slate: The Modern Denial of Human Nature. Viking, 2002

Shubin, Neil. Your Inner Fish: A Journey into the 3.5-Billion-Year History of the Human Body. Pantheon Books, 2008

Wright, Robert. The Moral Animal: Why We Are the Way We Are: The New Science of Evolutionary Psychology. Vintage Books, 1994

Chapter Nine

Axelrod, Robert. The Evolution of Cooperation. Basic Books, 1984.

Boyd, Robert, and Peter J. Richerson. The Origin and Evolution of Cultures. Oxford University Press, 2005.

De Waal, Frans. The Bonobo and the Atheist: In Search of Humanism Among the Primates. W. W. Norton & Company, 2013.

De Waal, Frans. Good Natured: The Origins of Right and Wrong in Humans and Other Animals. Harvard University Press, 1996.

Harari, Yuval Noah. Sapiens: A Brief History of Humankind. Harper, 2015.

Morris, Desmond. The Naked Ape: A Zoologist's Study of the Human Animal. Dell Publishing, 1967.

Nowak, Martin A. Evolutionary Dynamics: Exploring the Equations of Life. Belknap Press of Harvard University Press, 2006.

Pinker, Steven. The Blank Slate: The Modern Denial of Human Nature. Viking, 2002.

Shubin, Neil. Your Inner Fish: A Journey into the 3. 5-Billion-Year History of the Human Body. Pantheon Books, 2008.

Wright, Robert. The Moral Animal: Why We Are the Way We Are: The New Science of Evolutionary Psychology. Vintage Books, 1994.

Chapter Ten

Axelrod, Robert. The Evolution of Cooperation. Basic Books, 1984.

Boyd, Robert, and Peter J. Richerson. The Origin and Evolution of Cultures. Oxford University Press, 2005.

De Waal, Frans. The Bonobo and the Atheist: In Search of Humanism Among the Primates. W. W. Norton & Company, 2013.

De Waal, Frans. Good Natured: The Origins of Right and Wrong in Humans and Other Animals. Harvard University Press, 1996.

Harari, Yuval Noah. Sapiens: A Brief History of Humankind. Harper, 2015.

Morris, Desmond. The Naked Ape: A Zoologist's Study of the Human Animal. Dell Publishing, 1967.

Nowak, Martin A. Evolutionary Dynamics: Exploring the Equations of Life. Belknap Press of Harvard University Press, 2006.

Pinker, Steven. The Blank Slate: The Modern Denial of Human Nature. Viking, 2002.

Shubin, Neil. Your Inner Fish: A Journey into the 3.5-Billion-Year History of the Human Body. Pantheon Books, 2008.

Wright, Robert. The Moral Animal: Why We Are the Way We Are: The New Science of Evolutionary Psychology. Vintage Books, 1994.

Chapter Eleven

Axelrod, Robert. The Evolution of Cooperation. Basic Books, 1984.

Boyd, Robert, and Peter J. Richerson. The Origin and Evolution of Cultures. Oxford University Press, 2005.

De Waal, Frans. The Bonobo and the Atheist: In Search of Humanism Among the Primates. W. W. Norton & Company, 2013.

De Waal, Frans. Good Natured: The Origins of Right and Wrong in Humans and Other Animals. Harvard University Press, 1996.

Harari, Yuval Noah. Sapiens: A Brief History of Humankind. Harper, 2015.

Morris, Desmond. The Naked Ape: A Zoologist's Study of the Human Animal. Dell Publishing, 1967.

Nowak, Martin A. Evolutionary Dynamics: Exploring the Equations of Life. Belknap Press of Harvard University Press, 2006.

Pinker, Steven. The Blank Slate: The Modern Denial of Human Nature. Viking, 2002.

Shubin, Neil. Your Inner Fish: A Journey into the 3. 5-Billion-Year History of the Human Body. Pantheon Books, 2008.

Wright, Robert. The Moral Animal: Why We Are the Way We Are: The New Science of Evolutionary Psychology. Vintage Books, 1994.

Chomsky, Noam. Manufacturing Consent: The Political Economy of the Mass Media. Pantheon Books, 1988.)

Achen, Christopher H., and Larry M. Bartels. Democracy for Realists: Why Elections Do Not Produce Responsive Government. Princeton University Press, 2016

Iyengar, Shanto, and Kyle Dropp. The Nature of Partisan Polarization: An Overview. Annual Review of Political Science, 2017.

Mann, Thomas E., and Norman J. Ornstein. It's Even Worse Than It Looks: How the American Constitutional System Collided With the New Politics of Extremism. Basic Books, 2012

Frank, Thomas. What's the Matter with Kansas? How Conservatives Won the Heart of America. Metropolitan Books, 2004

Chapter Twelve

Bourdieu, Pierre. [Relevant Work on Social Capital, Habitus, or Distinction]. [Publisher], [Year].

Chomsky, Noam. Manufacturing Consent: The Political Economy of the Mass Media. Pantheon Books, 1988.

Darwin, Charles. On the Origin of Species. John Murray, 1859. (Often used for "Survival of the Fittest" in a broader social context).

Diamond, Jared. Guns, Germs, and Steel: The Fates of Human Societies. W. W. Norton & Company, 1997.

Foucault, Michel. Discipline and Punish: The Birth of the Prison. Pantheon Books, 1977. (For Power/Knowledge, Disciplinary Society).

Friedman, Milton. Capitalism and Freedom. University of Chicago Press, 1962. (For Shareholder Primacy, Free Market Capitalism).

Gramsci, Antonio. Selections from the Prison Notebooks. International Publishers, 1971. (For Cultural Hegemony).

Hobbes, Thomas. Leviathan. 1651.

Klein, Naomi. The Shock Doctrine: The Rise of Disaster Capitalism. Metropolitan Books, 2007.

Machiavelli, Niccolò. The Prince. 1532.

Marx, Karl. Das Kapital. 1867. (For Class Struggle, Economic Power Dynamics).

Michels, Robert. Political Parties: A Sociological Study of the Oligarchical Tendencies of Modern Democracy. Hearst's International Library Co., 1915.

Mosca, Gaetano. The Ruling Class. McGraw-Hill, 1939.

Olson, Mancur. The Logic of Collective Action: Public Goods and the Theory of Groups. Harvard University Press, 1965. (For Rent-Seeking).

Pareto, Vilfredo. The Mind and Society: A Treatise on General Sociology. Harcourt, Brace and Company, 1935. (For Elite Theory, Circulation of Elites).

Rodney, Walter. How Europe Underdeveloped Africa. Howard University Press, 1972.

Various authors in Behavioral Economics & Cognitive Psychology. [General Reference to key texts in these fields, e.g., "Thinking, Fast and Slow" by Daniel Kahneman, "Nudge" by Richard Thaler and Cass Sunstein]. [Publisher], [Year].

Wallerstein, Immanuel. The Modern World-System. Academic Press, 1974.

Weber, Max. Economy and Society: An Outline of Interpretive Sociology. University of California Press, 1978. (For Power, Authority, Social Stratification).

Chapter Thirteen

Akerlof, George A., and Robert J. Shiller. Phishing for Phools: The Economics of Manipulation and Deception. Princeton University Press, 2015.

Berman, Sarah Michelle. Don't Call It a Cult: The Shocking Story of Keith Raniere and the Women of NXIVM. Viking, 2021.

Cialdini, Robert B.. Influence: The Psychology of Persuasion. HarperBusiness, 2006.

Dawkins, Richard. The Selfish Gene. Oxford University Press, 1976.

Frank, Robert H.. Success and Luck: Good Fortune and the Myth of Meritocracy. Princeton University Press, 2016.

Goffman, Erving. The Presentation of Self in Everyday Life. Doubleday, 1959.

Goleman, Daniel. Social Intelligence: The New Science of Human Relationships. Bantam Books, 2006.

Guinn, Jeff. The Road to Jonestown: Jim Jones and Peoples Temple. Simon & Schuster, 2017.

Hamilton, W. D.. "The Genetical Evolution of Social Behaviour. I." Journal of Theoretical Biology, vol. 7, no. 1, 1964, pp. 1-16.

Hardin, Garrett. "The Tragedy of the Commons." Science, vol. 162, no. 3859, 1968, pp. 1243-48.

Hofstede, Geert. Culture's Consequences: International Differences in Work-Related Values. Sage Publications, 1980.

Kahneman, Daniel. Thinking, Fast and Slow. Farrar, Straus and Giroux, 2011.

Kaplan, David E., and Andrew Marshall. The Cult at the End of the World: The Terrifying Story of the Aum Doomsday Cult, from the Subways of Tokyo to the Nuclear Arsenals of Russia. Crown, 1996.

Lifton, Robert Jay. Thought Reform and the Psychology of Totalism: A Study of "Brainwashing" in China. University of North Carolina Press, 1989.

Mackay, Charles. Extraordinary Popular Delusions and the Madness of Crowds. Harmony Books, 1980.

Massingale, Kelley. "The Rise and Fall of NXIVM: A Social Network Analysis." 2023. Simon Fraser University, MA thesis. SFU Library Thesis Template, summit.sfu.ca/_flysystem/fedora/2023-09/etd22686.pdf. Accessed 27 June 2025.

Meadows, Donella H., et al. The Limits to Growth. Universe Books, 1972.

Morris, Desmond. The Naked Ape: A Zoologist's Study of the Human Animal. Dell Publishing, 1967.

"NXIVM." Wikipedia, Wikimedia Foundation, 26 June 2025, en.wikipedia.org/wiki/NXIVM. Accessed 27 June 2025.

Pinker, Steven. The Blank Slate: The Modern Denial of Human Nature. Penguin Books, 2002.

Rachels, James. The Elements of Moral Philosophy. McGraw-Hill, 2003.

Sapolsky, Robert M.. Behave: The Biology of Humans at Our Best and Worst. Penguin Press, 2017.

Schein, Edgar H.. Coercive Persuasion: A Socio-Psychological Analysis of Brainwashing of American Civilian Prisoners by the Chinese Communists. W.W. Norton & Company, 1961.

Shimazono, Susumu. "In the Wake of Aum." Japanese Journal of Religious Studies, vol. 22, no. 3-4, 1995, pp. 381-411.

Singer, Margaret T.. "Cults, Coercion, and Contumely." Cultic Studies Journal, vol. 12, no. 1, 1995, pp. 24-42.

Smith, Adam. The Wealth of Nations. 1776. (Various modern editions, e.g., University of Chicago Press, 1976.)

Tomasello, Michael. The Cultural Origins of Human Cognition. Harvard University Press, 1999.

Trivers, Robert L.. "The Evolution of Reciprocal Altruism." The Quarterly Review of Biology, vol. 46, no. 1, 1971, pp. 35-57.

Tversky, Amos, and Daniel Kahneman. Choices, Values, and Frames. Cambridge University Press, 2000.

VanBaale, Kali White. "The NXIVM Cult: An Inside Look at the Classes and Cruelty." A&E True Crime, A+E Global Media, 11 May 2021, www.aetv.com/real-crime/nxivm-cult. Accessed 27 June 2025.

The Vow. Created by Jehane Noujaim and Karim Amer. HBO, 2020-2022.

Wilson, Edward O.. Sociobiology: The New Synthesis. Harvard University Press, 1975.

Zimbardo, Philip G.. The Lucifer Effect: Understanding How Good People Turn Evil. Random

Chapter Fourteen

Akerlof, George A., and Robert J. Shiller. Phishing for Phools: The Economics of Manipulation and Deception. Princeton University Press, 2015.

Axelrod, Robert. The Evolution of Cooperation. Basic Books, 1984.

Berman, Sarah Michelle. Don't Call It a Cult: The Shocking Story of Keith Raniere and the Women of NXIVM. Viking, 2021.

Boehm, Christopher. Hierarchy in the Forest: The Evolution of Egalitarian Behavior. Harvard University Press, 1999.

Bowles, Samuel, and Herbert Gintis. A Cooperative Species: Human Reciprocity and Its Evolution. Princeton University Press, 2011.

Camerer, Colin F.. Behavioral Game Theory: Experiments in Strategic Interaction. Princeton University Press, 2003.

Churchland, Patricia S.. Braintrust: What Neuroscience Tells Us about Morality. Princeton University Press, 2011.

Cialdini, Robert B.. Influence: The Psychology of Persuasion. HarperBusiness, 2006.

Cosmides, Leda, and John Tooby. "Evolutionary Psychology: A Primer." Center for Evolutionary Psychology, 1997, www.cep.ucsb.edu/primer.html. Accessed 27 June 2025.

Darwin, Charles. The Descent of Man, and Selection in Relation to Sex. John Murray, 1871.

Dawkins, Richard. The Selfish Gene. Oxford University Press, 1976.

de Waal, Frans B. M.. Chimpanzee Politics: Power and Sex among Apes. Johns Hopkins University Press, 1982.

---. Good Natured: The Origins of Right and Wrong in Humans and Other Animals. Harvard University Press, 1996.

---. Our Inner Ape: A Leading Primatologist Explains Why We Are Who We Are. Riverhead Books, 2005.

---. The Bonobo and the Atheist: In Search of Humanism Among the Primates. W. W. Norton & Company, 2013.

Diamond, Jared. Guns, Germs, and Steel: The Fates of Human Societies. W. W. Norton & Company, 1997.

Fehr, Ernst, and Urs Fischbacher. "The Nature of Human Altruism." Nature, vol. 425, no. 6960, 2003, pp. 785-91.

Fiske, Alan P.. Structures of Social Life: The Four Elementary Forms of Human Relations. Free Press, 1992.

Frank, Robert H.. Passions Within Reason: The Strategic Role of the Emotions. W. W. Norton & Company, 1988.

---. Success and Luck: Good Fortune and the Myth of Meritocracy. Princeton University Press, 2016.

Gintis, Herbert. Game Theory Evolving: A Problem-Centered Introduction to Modeling Strategic Interaction. Princeton University Press, 2009.

Goffman, Erving. The Presentation of Self in Everyday Life. Doubleday, 1959.

Goleman, Daniel. Social Intelligence: The New Science of Human Relationships. Bantam Books, 2006.

Gough, Kathleen. "The Kula Ring: A Reinterpretation." Man, vol. 59, 1959, pp. 171-76.

Guinn, Jeff. The Road to Jonestown: Jim Jones and Peoples Temple. Simon & Schuster, 2017.

Hauser, Marc D.. Moral Minds: How Nature Designed Our Universal Sense of Right and Wrong. Ecco, 2006.

Hamilton, W. D.. "The Genetical Evolution of Social Behaviour. I." Journal of Theoretical Biology, vol. 7, no. 1, 1964, pp. 1-16.

Hardin, Garrett. "The Tragedy of the Commons." Science, vol. 162, no. 3859, 1968, pp. 1243-48.

Henrich, Joseph. The Secret of Our Success: How Culture Is Driving Human Evolution, Domesticating Our Species, and Making Us Smarter. Princeton University Press, 2016.

Hofstede, Geert. Culture's Consequences: International Differences in Work-Related Values. Sage Publications, 1980.

Hrdy, Sarah Blaffer. Mothers and Others: The Evolutionary Origins of Mutual Understanding. Belknap Press of Harvard University Press, 2009.

Joyce, Richard. The Evolution of Morality. MIT Press, 2006.

Kahneman, Daniel. Thinking, Fast and Slow. Farrar, Straus and Giroux, 2011.

Kaplan, David E., and Andrew Marshall. The Cult at the End of the World: The Terrifying Story of the Aum Doomsday Cult, from the Subways of Tokyo to the Nuclear Arsenals of Russia. Crown, 1996.

Kropotkin, Peter. Mutual Aid: A Factor of Evolution. 1902. (Various modern editions, e.g., Dover Publications, 2006.)

Lévi-Strauss, Claude. The Elementary Structures of Kinship. Beacon Press, 1969.

Madden, Amy. The Evolution of Empathy: Why We Care and How We Cooperate. Oxford University Press, 2018.

Mauss, Marcel. The Gift: Forms and Functions of Exchange in Archaic Societies. W. W. Norton & Company, 1990.

Massingale, Kelley. "The Rise and Fall of NXIVM: A Social Network Analysis." 2023. Simon Fraser University, MA thesis. SFU Library Thesis Template, summit.sfu.ca/_flysystem/fedora/2023-09/etd22686.pdf. Accessed 27 June 2025.

Meadows, Donella H., et al. The Limits to Growth. Universe Books, 1972.

Morris, Desmond. The Naked Ape: A Zoologist's Study of the Human Animal. Dell Publishing, 1967.

"NXIVM." Wikipedia, Wikimedia Foundation, 26 June 2025, en.wikipedia.org/wiki/NXIVM. Accessed 27 June 2025.

Ostrom, Elinor. Governing the Commons: The Evolution of Institutions for Collective Action. Cambridge University Press, 1990.

Pinker, Steven. The Blank Slate: The Modern Denial of Human Nature. Penguin Books, 2002.

Rachels, James. The Elements of Moral Philosophy. McGraw-Hill, 2003.

Sapolsky, Robert M.. Behave: The Biology of Humans at Our Best and Worst. Penguin Press, 2017.

Schein, Edgar H.. Coercive Persuasion: A Socio-Psychological Analysis of Brainwashing of American Civilian Prisoners by the Chinese Communists. W.W. Norton & Company, 1961.

Shimazono, Susumu. "In the Wake of Aum." Japanese Journal of Religious Studies, vol. 22, no. 3-4, 1995, pp. 381-411.

Singer, Margaret T.. "Cults, Coercion, and Contumely." Cultic Studies Journal, vol. 12, no. 1, 1995, pp. 24-42.

Smith, Adam. The Theory of Moral Sentiments. 1759.

---. The Wealth of Nations. 1776. (Various modern editions, e.g., University of Chicago Press, 1976.)

Sober, Elliott, and David Sloan Wilson. Unto Others: The Evolution and Psychology of Unselfish Behavior. Harvard University Press, 1998.

Tomasello, Michael. A Natural History of Human Morality. Harvard University Press, 2016.

---. The Cultural Origins of Human Cognition. Harvard University Press, 1999.

---. Why We Cooperate. MIT Press, 2009.

Trivers, Robert L.. "The Evolution of Reciprocal Altruism." The Quarterly Review of Biology, vol. 46, no. 1, 1971, pp. 35-57.

---. Social Evolution. Benjamin/Cummings, 1985.

Turiel, Elliot. The Culture of Morality: Social Development, Context, and Conflict. Cambridge University Press, 2002.

VanBaale, Kali White. "The NXIVM Cult: An Inside Look at the Classes and Cruelty." A&E True Crime, A+E Global Media, 11 May 2021, www.aetv.com/real-crime/nxivm-cult. Accessed 27 June 2025.

The Vow. Created by Jehane Noujaim and Karim Amer. HBO, 2020-2022.

Wilson, Edward O.. On Human Nature. Harvard University Press, 1978.

---. Sociobiology: The New Synthesis. Harvard University Press, 1975.

Zimbardo, Philip G.. The Lucifer Effect: Understanding How Good People Turn Evil. Random House, 2007.

Chapter Fifteen

Pierre Boulle Planet of the Apes (Original novel and subsequent film series for thematic inspiration and imagery)

Jared Diamond Collapse: How Societies Choose to Fail or Succeed (For historical examples of resource depletion and societal breakdown, e.g., Easter Island, Maya, Rome)

Yuval Noah Harari Sapiens: A Brief History of Humankind (For narratives of human dominance and impact on ecosystems, future technological trajectories)

Naomi Klein This Changes Everything: Capitalism vs. The Climate (For critique of economic systems driving environmental destruction)

Thomas Malthus An Essay on the Principle of Population (For foundational ideas on population growth and resource limits)

Garrett Hardin The Tragedy of the Commons (For the concept of shared resource depletion due to individual self-interest)

Paul R. Ehrlich The Population Bomb (For concerns about resource scarcity and overpopulation)

The Club of Rome The Limits to Growth (Early modeling of resource depletion and societal collapse)

Carl Sagan Cosmos (For broader perspectives on human civilization's fragility, the pale blue dot)

Robert Axelrod The Evolution of Cooperation (For how cooperation can arise, but how defection can also dominate under certain conditions)

Elinor Ostrom Governing the Commons (For successful, but complex, strategies to avoid resource depletion)

Adam Smith The Wealth of Nations (Invisible Hand, Self-Interest in Markets – how its unchecked pursuit leads to unintended consequences)

Chapter Sixteen

Axelrod, Robert. The Evolution of Cooperation. Basic Books, 1984.

Buss, David M. The Evolution of Desire: Strategies of Human Mating. Basic Books, 1994.

Carr, E. H. The Twenty Years' Crisis, 1919-1939: An Introduction to the Study of International Relations. Palgrave Macmillan, 2001. (Original work published 1939).

Dawkins, Richard. The Selfish Gene. Oxford University Press, 1976.

Greene, Joshua D. Moral Tribes: Emotion, Reason, and the Gap Between Us and Them. Penguin Press, 2013.

Harari, Yuval Noah. Sapiens: A Brief History of Humankind. Harper, 2015.

Hobbes, Thomas. Leviathan. Edited by C. B. Macpherson, Penguin Classics, 1968. (Original work published 1651).

Machiavelli, Niccolò. The Prince. Translated by Harvey C. Mansfield, University of Chicago Press, 1998. (Original work published 1532).

Morgenthau, Hans J. Politics Among Nations: The Struggle for Power and Peace. Alfred A. Knopf, 1948.

Pinker, Steven. The Blank Slate: The Modern Denial of Human Nature. Viking, 2002.

Sapolsky, Robert M. Behave: The Biology of Humans at Our Best and Worst. Penguin Press, 2017.

Smith, Adam. The Wealth of Nations. Edited by Edwin Cannan, Random House, 1937. (Original work published 1776).

Wright, Robert. The Moral Animal: Why We Are the Way We Are. Pantheon Books, 1994.

Chapter Seventeen

Axelrod, Robert. The Evolution of Cooperation. Basic Books, 1984.

Buss, David M. The Evolution of Desire: Strategies of Human Mating. Basic Books, 1994.

Carr, E. H. The Twenty Years' Crisis, 1919-1939: An Introduction to the Study of International Relations. Palgrave Macmillan, 2001. (Original work published 1939).

Dawkins, Richard. The Selfish Gene. Oxford University Press, 1976.

Greene, Joshua D. Moral Tribes: Emotion, Reason, and the Gap Between Us and Them. Penguin Press, 2013.

Harari, Yuval Noah. Sapiens: A Brief History of Humankind. Harper, 2015.

Hobbes, Thomas. Leviathan. Edited by C. B. Macpherson, Penguin Classics, 1968. (Original work published 1651).

Machiavelli, Niccolò. The Prince. Translated by Harvey C. Mansfield, University of Chicago Press, 1998. (Original work published 1532).

Morgenthau, Hans J. Politics Among Nations: The Struggle for Power and Peace. Alfred A. Knopf, 1948.

Pinker, Steven. The Blank Slate: The Modern Denial of Human Nature. Viking, 2002.

Sapolsky, Robert M. Behave: The Biology of Humans at Our Best and Worst. Penguin Press, 2017.

Smith, Adam. The Wealth of Nations. Edited by Edwin Cannan, Random House, 1937. (Original work published 1776).

Chapter Eighteen

Sadly, all that is mentioned in this chapter was personally experienced in 77 years by the author. None of these experiences were wasted as without them the

ideas in this book would have never coalesced. Life is
a dark ride and even darker for some.

Index